A Sociolinguistic Insight into the Italian Community in the UK:
Workplace Language as an Identity Marker

A Sociolinguistic Insight into the Italian Community in the UK: Workplace Language as an Identity Marker

By

Siria Guzzo

With a Preface by David Britain

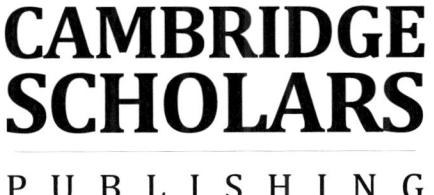

CAMBRIDGE
SCHOLARS
PUBLISHING

A Sociolinguistic Insight into the Italian Community in the UK:
Workplace Language as an Identity Marker,
by Siria Guzzo

This book was first published in 2014

Cambridge Scholars Publishing

12 Back Chapman Street, Newcastle upon Tyne, NE6 2XX, UK

British Library Cataloguing in Publication Data
A catalogue record for this book is available from the British Library

ISBN (10): 1-4438-6674-1, ISBN (13): 978-1-4438-6674-3

Dedicated to my beloved grandparents.

TABLE OF CONTENTS

LIST OF ILLUSTRATIONS

LIST OF TABLES

AUTHORS' NOTE

The present work is based on research on the Bedford Italian Community which was partly divulgated through various previously published articles. I wish to express my heartfelt thanks to CSP for their very kind invitation to publish the work in a new book form and allow the research contained within to become accessible to a wider audience.

The nature of the vast British Italian community means that the study published in this volume represents only the beginning of a journey. Since this research was first carried out in 2004, I have had the opportunity to extend the work on Bedford to embrace observations of the Italian community of Peterborough, especially the 3rd generation, some of whose findings I have tried to integrate into the concluding remarks of the present study.

I hope in the future, however, to be able to go further and deeper into the analysis of the speech community, and look forward to the day when observations on British Italian communities in Bletchley, Loughborough and further northward as far as Scotland can add breadth and depth to the studies I have so far had the great fortune, and privilege to begin.

PREFACE

In the very earliest sociolinguistic studies of American speech communities, for example, Labov's work on Martha's Vineyard (1963) and the Lower East Side of New York (1966/2006), and Shuy, Wolfram and Riley's studies of Detroit (1967), ethnicity was considered to play a very significant role in how variation in English was patterned. In Britain, however, research on ethnic variation in English remained largely unexplored until very recent times, with virtually no work on the structural characteristics of ethnic dialects of British English appearing beyond those of the Caribbean diaspora community.

The beginning of this century has seen a number of studies, however, which have begun to rectify this gap in the literature. First, we can point to Sue Fox's work in Tower Hamlets in East London (e.g. 2003, 2007). She examined, through a very sensitive ethnographic study of members of a youth club, how accent features of local Bangladeshi English were being diffused to the Anglo community via close social network ties. This study was able to shed light, therefore, not just on the characteristics of London Bangladeshi English, but also on the interethnic transmission of linguistic change.

Two large scale surveys of ethnic variation in London English followed (e.g. Cheshire, Kerswill, Fox and Torgersen 2011) which highlighted the scale and extent of the transmission of both phonological and grammatical features from London's more recent migrant communities to the Anglo population, and proposed that a pan-ethnic variety – Multicultural London English – was in the process of focussing. Now, many further studies are emerging of language variation in the English of migrant communities in Britain – for example, Sharma's (e.g. 2011) work on the Indian community of London, Khan's (2007) research on the Caribbean, Pakistani and Anglo communities of Birmingham; Alam's (2007) study of Asian Englishes in Glasgow and Kirkham (2011)'s work on the Pakistani community in Sheffield. Still very much under-researched, however, are the indigenising English varieties of Britain's earlier immigrant communities. There has, for example, been an Italian community in Britain for over seven hundred years (King 1977: 176). Up until the reformation, many financiers, medics, craftspeople and clerics, especially in London, were of Italian descent. By the end of the 19th century there were over 20,000 Italians in the country. The two decades after World War II were the most significant, however, for Italian migration to the UK. King (1977: 178) shows that in the two decades after 1948 almost 150,000 Italians came to settle in the UK (despite the weather).

For various statistical and institutional reasons, it is hard to gain accurate information about the Italian population today: in the last census of 2011 almost 100, 000 people in England and Wales claimed Italian as their "main language", 125,000 claimed Italian was their ethnic group, but well over 130,000 had been born in Italy. Kyambi (2005a: 51-52) highlights the geographical concentrations of *recent* migrants from Italy, especially in London, but because the census only assesses migrants who have arrived within the 10 years previous to the count, it gives only very poor indications of the present size of longer established migrant communities. There have been, until now, just a couple of brief (macro-) sociolinguistic overviews of the British Italian community (e.g. Linguistic Minorities Project 1985; Cervi 1991), but very few studies specifically examining the structural characteristics of their English.

Dr Siria Guzzo's examination, in this volume, of the English of Bedford's Italian community, therefore, is extremely timely, both in examining a neglected yet significant migrant population in Great Britain, and in terms of adding to what we know about the ethnic diversity of British English. It also, importantly, provides an important case study of ethnic variation *outside* of the major urban conurbations where multicultural Englishes have been examined thus far.

Guzzo's study, as well as examining a couple of the more generic variables that many studies investigate, considers a number of features which provide an opportunity for the speakers in her study to specifically index their Italian identities – such as the use of /a/ in foreign (often Italian) loan words, such as "pasta", and the Anglicisation of other Italian lexical items – as well as features that examine the extent to which second language features of Italian learners of English have become indigenised amongst second and third generation British Italians, such as a relative lack of inversion in question formation, and third person present tense zero. She also, like few other studies on ethnic variation in British English, takes an intergenerational approach, tracking features from first generation migrants to third generation locals, providing a fascinating insight into how the process of indigenisation, alongside other variable social and linguistic factors, shapes language variation.

Much work is still to be done on the sociolinguistics of this significant and long-standing migrant community (as well as on many other migrant communities) and Guzzo herself has expanded her explorations of British

Italian English in recent work on the community in Peterborough. The work presented here, however, represents an important first step in understanding what happens (socio)linguistically and dialectologically when Italians make Britain their home.

David Britain
(Bern)

ACKNOWLEDGEMENTS

There are many people I wish to thank for their invaluable help in the production of this work.

First and foremost I would like to express my thanks to the Italian community of Bedford, without whose support this study would not have been possible. Not only did they give me their cooperation, they also accepted me wholeheartedly into their community and offered their sincere friendship. The massive amount of information they put at my disposal is something I treasure, and I consider myself privileged to have received their hospitality and constant help. I thank each and every one of the businesses I was able to record: the Cappuccino Bar, Mrs Maria Chirico and her beautiful family, La Rondine, AB Fruits, Santaniello's pizza house, La Dolce Vita, the hairdressers Tony, Rocco, Vincenzo and Giovanni, and above all my dearest friends Salvatore Garganese and his sister Elisabetta, Cinzia Iacono, Christina Spiniello and her lovely family, Liberato Lionetti and his precious staff.

Moreover, I also felt most privileged to have received the external supervision of Prof Dr David Britain. I am deeply grateful for his constant and thoughtful advice on every aspect of my work, for sharing his incomparable knowledge with me, and for his caring support. To him I owe special thanks for believing in me and my research.

For her work on the history of the Italian community in Britain, on which I have been heavily reliant for the first section of this work, I owe a great debt of gratitude to Terri Colpi. I offer the same deep gratitude to Charles Boberg for his inspiration about the analysis of foreign (a), which was of immense importance to my research and in much of what I have tried to show in Chapter Three.

I am extremely thankful to my family and friends for supporting me throughout these demanding years. Special thanks to Gina Di Muro for her expert advice and friendship. Thanks especially to my brother for his invaluable help which has proved to be crucial with any and all technical problems. I thank my Mum and Dad for being there for me on all occasions. Special thanks go to my Gran and Grandpa for shining down on me from Heaven.

Last but not least, I am eternally grateful to my husband Fabrizio for his priceless psychological support, his patient help, and for tolerating my frequent states of despair, and to my darling son Matteo for always brightening up my days and giving me endless love. Thank you all!

INTRODUCTION

Like many other Western societies, Britain is undergoing significant social changes, many of which are caused by migrations and the transnationalisation of social and family life. The migration of peoples and cross-cultural encounters, while sometimes giving rise to a challenging coexistence, nevertheless enhance the contemporary relocation of cultures and languages, resulting in new linguistic outcomes. The construction of hybrid[1] speech communities is a difficult cultural process whose consequences are often ambiguous and heterogeneous. Language plays a major role in the birth of new forms of communication, encouraged by processes of self-construction, self-conscious investigation, and the growth of new social representations. As Candlin and Gotti (2004: 5) observe,

"Language is approached here as inseparable from a given socio-cultural configuration – not merely consistent with it, but deeply involved in its construction of reality and its representations. From single phrases to generic patterns, linguistic constructs encode a culture-bound world view".

Moreover, as Bell (2001:164) claims,

"A part of our behaviour is a reflection of the social characteristics of groups we are associated with. However, categories such as ethnicity have fluid boundaries, and people's definition of their own ethnicity may even change in different situations".

People are not static entities and the language they use in specific situations or contexts cannot be regarded as fixed and never-changing (cf. Duranti and Goodwin 1992). There are norms for different situations and groups, and as a result, a particular style can be used to conform to a context, to create a situation, or to respond to a specific audience type.

---

[1] The term *hybrid* is used here with reference to the convergence of different cultures generated by geographical displacements. In order to avoid the reproduction of ambiguous categories of the past, *hybridity* assumes here a theoretical perspective which denies circumscribing identity in a conservative framework so as to acknowledge the development of new multiple models of cultural blending and representation.

In light of these observations, the situation of Bedford Italians in Britain provides an interesting case study. From the 1950s, and for the following decade, thousands of Italians most of whom originally from Southern Italy, arrived in the town of Bedford, attracted by the offer of employment in the local brick works factory. The London brick industry was in desperate need of labour at the time and the world's largest and most well known brick factory, Marston Valley Bricks Co. was hard pushed to find English labourers willing to work in the brickfield (King and King 1977, Cavallaro 1981, Colpi 1991). Meanwhile, there were Italians in desperate need of work and ready to seize any and all opportunities in order to earn money to support their families.

More than 10,000 Italians settled in Bedford and in the surrounding area from the 1950s onwards and this gave rise to a diaspora community spanning three generations (Kyambi 2005b). According to the 2001 census, 2 in 7 of Bedford's population are of Italian origin, which means that 28% of all Bedfordians belong to the Bedford Italian Community (BIC). In an earlier study, and by means of a questionnaire, it became clear that the BIC was a composite hybrid community, and that there was quite a significant use of the Italian language within it. Their ethnic identity is extremely strong and is perceived as Italian rather than British or English, and although English is the first language of the vast majority of 2nd and 3rd generation BIs, most have at least good passive competence in the Italian spoken by their parents and grandparents (Guzzo 2005, 2007).

In an attempt to gain a more thorough understanding of the linguistic and ethnic identity of the BIC, special attention is paid in this study to the concept of the feeling of 'Italianness' perceived within the community. The language spoken by BIs is also investigated in an attempt to map any changes that have occurred over time and across generations. Another objective of this research is to discover whether the linguistic distinctiveness of this speech community is used to signal ethnic identity in the language used in the workplace in particular.

In order to explore the linguistic mechanisms underlying minority languages, information is provided about the way language is used in a dataset of three workplaces of one of the largest Italian communities in the UK, and per capita, in the world. This study highlights the importance of a sociolinguistic examination of English in service encounters, it applies an audience design approach and uses accommodation theory. It focuses on the relationship between ethnicity and code choice with the aim of drawing attention to the social changes that are taking place in the representation of new hybrid identities in order to contribute to the understanding of the language of the Italian diaspora. The methodology used is based on participant observation, direct data collection, ethnographic audio recordings, and a descriptive approach based on qualitative and quantitative analysis. As for the social variables, all three generations of Bedford Italians are taken into account in order to examine variation according to age. In addition, in order to research inter- and intra-speaker variation following an "audience design" approach (Bell 1984), the variables of context with regard to the workplace setting are considered, and also whether the interlocutors are Italian or British.

From earlier results it became clear that further investigation of the language of Bedford Italians was needed, and by applying an audience design approach while also examining the use of ethnic-based language in the workplace, new research questions have emerged.

Specifically, the present study tests some hypotheses:

1. Does the specific context under scrutiny, that is the workplace, influence the language of Bedford Italians?
2. Focusing on inter- and intra- speaker variation and investigating L2 features in specific contexts, does the ethnic identity of the interlocutors have an impact on the language used?
3. Does audience design give birth to a special type of English Bedford Italian, which Italians tend to use at work as a form of ESP?
4. Do Italians Anglicise Italian lexical items when speaking to British people, whether they are colleagues or customers? Can we hypothesize the existence of "phonological code-switching" leading Italians to shift in the workplace?

There is a significant number of Italians in the UK and they have a long and complex migration history. However, there is scant literature compared to the Italian diasporas in the US, Australia, Canada and Latin America. Ethnically, Bedford is one of the most highly mixed communities in Britain and is home to over a hundred immigrant languages, in which Italian finds itself alongside Punjabi, Turkish, Polish, Portuguese, Cantonese and Mandarin Chinese. Immigrants from over 50 different countries have settled in Bedford over the past few decades: Polish migrants arrived immediately after World War II, Italians started moving in the 1950s and continued throughout the following decade along with Indians, West Indians and Pakistanis who joined the other minority groups (Tosi 1984). For all these communities of migrants who have settled in Bedford over the years, the words of Allan Bell hold true:

> "We are not a *tabula rasa*. We bring to the present the shapings of our past, of our relationships, of our environment. Yet we are more than the sum of those things". (Allan Bell, 2001:164)

CHAPTER ONE

ITALIANS AND ITALIAN IN BRITAIN: A HISTORY

1.1 Italians in Bedford, UK

Italian immigration to Bedford began in 1951, and continued until the end of the 1960s. Taking the sociolinguistic situation in Italy in those years into consideration, we can assume that the hundreds of thousands who came spoke one of the southern dialects as their first language, and Italian as their second. According to the 2001 census, two in 7 of Bedford's 150,000 inhabitants are of Italian origin and nowadays Bedford has the largest Italian community in the United Kingdom (Kyambi 2005b).

The literature on Italians in the UK is limited compared to Italian diasporas such as those in the US, Australia, Canada and Latin America. Existing studies describe a group which is "fragmented and heterogeneous with a long and complex migration history to Britain" (Fortier 2000, Palmer 1977, Sponza 1988 as in Zontini 2004), and most of the studies have concentrated on describing the evolution and features of this migration, tracing the formation of the first Italian communities, as in the studies of Colpi (1991), Cavallaro (1981) and King and King (1977).

The main reason why these people came to Britain was obviously not the weather; they migrated to escape abject poverty in most cases and hoped to make a decent living for themselves and their families. As a result, they seized the opportunity to work in British Industry. But migration is never a static process given that extended families, relatives and friends tend to become involved in what could be called a chain reaction. The migrant establishes a connection with the new environment, travelling back and forth between Italy and Britain and often those closest to the migrant also end up moving to the new land. This has been the case for generations of Italians who have emigrated to Britain from the nineteenth century to the present day.

1.2 Historical background of the Italian Community
of Bedford

Considering Great Britain as a whole, Italian immigration can be divided into two important phases: 1) a first stage at the turn of the nineteenth century when a large number of men began to arrive in the country and 2) in the years immediately after World War II, when real mass immigration began.

There is one phase involving a large group of writers, artists, and musicians who moved from Italy to settle in the United Kingdom, and another whose starting point is found around the 1820s and 1830s when there is a flux of the poorer peasant population. Of this second group, some were from Tuscany and Emilia Romagna, while others were from the Ciociaria countryside just north of the region of Naples. They were part of a great exodus of people in search of work (Colpi 1991).

They settled in London and Manchester, and formed the famous communities of "Little Italy" in Clerkenwell and Ancoats. On their arrival in Britain, they made a living as organ grinders, playing popular Italian songs on the streets. Before leaving Italy, it was obligatory for the migrants to have a contract with a *padrone* in Britain, and this 'master' would be in complete control of the immigrants regarding their work, food, and accommodation for the first two or three years after arrival. Once that time had passed, however, and their contractual obligations had been served out, they were free to work for themselves. They were able to continue earning money as organ grinders if they wished or they could take up other jobs of their choice (Colpi 1991, King and King 1977).

In addition to street musicians, skilled statuette makers and semi-skilled craftsmen came to London around the 1850s and spread out across the country. Two decades later, in the 1870s, men with more advanced skills, including knife sharpeners and mosaic workers as well as other skilled craftsmen, also migrated to Britain in the hope of having a better life (Colpi 1991).

With the decline of organ-grinding from the 1880s onwards, and the need to find new lines of work, Italians started to move into the catering sector. Continuing to operate as itinerant workers at first, their jobs changed with the seasons and they would sell roasted chestnuts in winter and ice-cream in summer in order to support their families. Some did well for themselves and by selling ice-cream on the streets they were able to make enough money to start their own businesses. Consequently, as more and more family members moved to Bedford to help run these businesses, the population of the Italian community saw its numbers triple. Thanks to their success, the community became more prosperous and several institutions were established. By the turn of the century the BIC had an Italian school, the Italian Church of St Peter's, the Mazzini Garibaldi Club, and an Italian Hospital (Colpi 1991).

During the 1900s, Italians migrated northwards and westwards from London, either settling in urban centres or smaller towns. In 1905, however, with the passage of the Aliens Act, the British government had to deal with very large waves of migration from Italy and, as a result, had to introduce important regulation. From that time onwards, the prospective migrant would have to make sure they had a job and accommodation in the United Kingdom before immigration could take place. Through strong connections, many were able to secure jobs and housing and entire families left their Italian villages. As a result of this chain migration, many towns came to have their own distinctive Italian communities in the UK.

Life in the two main Italian colonies of Clerkenwell and Ancoats had already taken on the appearance of a "Little Italy" when a third Italian colony was established in Soho, London. It thrived primarily thanks to the success of the catering trade. This was a new colony and was distinct from that of Clerkenwell. The Italians of Soho came mainly from Lombardy and Piedmont in the North of Italy, and found employment in the hotels, clubs and restaurants in the West End. Working in the more sophisticated environment "up West", they were often better paid. (Colpi 1991).

Many Italians began to really prosper as a result of their hard work. They had seized their opportunities, and substantial profits had been made. Many of them returned to Italy as rich men and women, and in so doing they set an example for their fellow townspeople to follow.

Unfortunately, with the outbreak of World War I, many 1st generation Italians left Britain and went back to Italy in order to join the army and to fight for their homeland. Since Italy and Great Britain were allies, however, many second generation Italians stayed behind and joined the British Armed Forces. When World War I finally ended, and having fought bravely for Britain, many of these brave soldiers returned as heroes. British Italians now had stability and economic prosperity. They had gained increasing respectability over the years, and a place in society. In the two decades after the war, a new golden era began for them.

Unfortunately, when World War II broke out, that golden era of stability and prosperity came to an abrupt end. With the rise of fascism, there was an attempt by the Italian government to regain control over the Italian communities that had spread throughout the world (Colpi 1991). The fascists attempted to tempt them back with an alluring range of activities including trips back to Italy. British Italians were happy to take part in these schemes and many did indeed return to their homeland. In 1940 however, Mussolini declared war on Britain and the Allies. This declaration caused attitudes to change and resulted in nationwide anti-Italian riots and demonstrations in the UK. Italian shops and cafés were targeted, looted and burned down. Italian families were assaulted by angry mobs and the integration and respectability built up over the years was no more. At government level, Churchill's governmental policy was ruthless, and the entire Italian male population was arrested. The consequences were tremendous: the Italian community was torn apart as a result and many businesses were forced to close. Male internment resulted in women and children being left unsupported and destitute, and many of them were forced to move away. For the Italians in Britain, this was a period of great hardship and distress.

Following the war, in the early 1950s, a second, crucial phase of Italian immigration to Great Britain began. Unlike the previous wave, this was real mass immigration and mainly consisted of workers recruited in bulk. After World War II, Great Britain had set out to rebuild its economy, and many sectors were in desperate need of new labour (Guzzo 2007). A major inter-governmental initiative had led to an agreement between the British Ministry of Labour and the Italian Government, and a bulk recruitment scheme offering jobs to a large number of Italian men and women had been set up in various industries where shortages had arisen. The first scheme brought over 2,000 young Italian women to work in the Lancashire cotton mills. Other Italians were offered coal mining jobs in Lancashire, Yorkshire and Derbyshire. Foundry workers were taken on at the same time in the Midlands, and tin-plate workers in Swansea (Colpi 1991).

The most significant flow of these migrants, however, arrived in the summer of 1951. The Italians among them were allocated to Bedfordshire brick factories, and in particular to the world's largest, Marston Valley Bricks Co., which had been faced with a grave shortage of English labourers.

As a result of this mass immigration throughout the 1950s and early 1960s, almost entire populations of southern Italian villages moved to Bedfordshire. One of the largest Italian communities was founded in the town of Bedford itself, along with similar communities in Peterborough, Bletchley, Loughborough, and Nottingham. The migrants to these towns originated from a great many villages along the length and breadth of Italy, but predominantly they came from the poorer southern regions of Campania, Apulia, Calabria and Sicily. This ongoing transferral of workers continued steadily over the years, and many new immigrants were still making their way to Britain at the end of the 1960s and at the beginning of the 1970s. Although many migrants belonging to this wave returned home within a few decades, Bedford today maintains a large southern Italian community which is still striking in its size, traditions, way of life, and governmental institutions (Guzzo 2007).

1.2.1 The social and cultural background of Italians in Britain

Immigration in the 1950s contributed to the establishment of different types of community. As they had in the past, many migrants arrived not only in Bedford, but also in London, Edinburgh, Glasgow and Manchester (Colpi 1991). Recruitment schemes requiring a work permit that had to be issued before entering the UK were initiated and strong connections with relatives and friends were of fundamental importance once again. The new wave of migrants came to the UK thanks to those who were already living and working there.

However, a change was taking place in the overall makeup of the British Italian community. In towns where "old" communities already existed, "new" communities were established. When this was the case, there was very little interaction between the two groups of Italians and to this day, fourth and fifth generation Italians whose ancestors arrived with the first wave of immigrants from the north of the country, claim to have very little in common with those who came from the south of Italy with the second wave in the 1950s. One explanation for this is that fourth and fifth generation Anglo-Italians tend to be well-educated and very successful and they are also well-integrated into the British system. The "new" immigrants, on the other hand, are from much poorer origins, did not have a proper education in most cases, and as a result, they are less sophisticated. The "old" areas of traditional occupation, primarily in catering, were taken over by the "new" immigrants who were culturally less refined than the previous generations of Italian settlers. What had been a chain-based migration up until that time was irreversibly changing into source village migration, dividing the history of the Italians in Great Britain into two culturally different flows (Colpi 1991).

As already mentioned, from 1951 to the end of the 1960s, thousands of Italian men arrived in groups to work in the Bedfordshire brickyards. But since the work was heavy, and it was not easy for those who had never worked in an industrial environment to adapt, many did not last long and were forced to go back to Italy. Thousands stayed, however, and made Bedford one of the largest and most important Italian communities in Britain. Nowadays, as many as 28% of Bedfordians are of Italian origin.

1.2.2 The social and territorial distribution of Bedford Italians

During the early 1950s, the first Italian colony of Bedford settled in the areas around Alexandra Road and Midland Road (see map below). Italian immigrants and their families found lodgings in the hostels around the brickfields and lived there for the first few years after their arrival. By 1958, more than half of the 5,000 Italians in the area were still living in conditions of poverty and in multiple occupation of those houses (Colpi 1991). By the late 1950s, however, the hard-working Bedford Italians had saved enough money to begin buying their own property, especially in the areas of Queens Park and Castle Road where the terraced houses were situated. By continuing to work tirelessly and never wasting their hard-earned money, they began to settle and finally prosper.

From a social perspective, throughout the 1960s the number of Italian community institutions grew significantly. Of particular note was the foundation of three new ethnic Italian churches, among which is the church of Santa Francesca Cabrini in Bedford. All three churches were established by the religious organisation of the Scalabrini Fathers. These churches have been central to the life of BI Italians as the focus of activity in the "new" communities, especially with regard to important milestones such as births, christenings, weddings and funerals. A large number of clubs and social events has developed around these churches, and made them the most important centre for Italian communities in Britain (Colpi 1991).

Traditionally, the role of family has always been much more important in people's social lives in Italy than it has in the UK. This tends to be even more the case in the south of Italy than in the north, and is still truer for a small village community than in a large metropolitan area. The same family traditions and values have also been cited when explaining the success of Italians in the catering trade. It is believed that the ability shown in running successful ethnic restaurants, coffee shops and ice-cream bars is thanks to family cohesion. Italian families in Bedford are bound together by kinship networks, and their community represents a sort of extended family. Ceremonies such as christenings, confirmations, engagements, marriages and funerals are important milestones in which extended Italian family networks gather together. Special occasions are not only considered important at a personal level, but they also signal the unity, wealth and loyalty of the community as a whole.

As in most villages in southern Italy, Patron Saints' Days and the traditional processions held on those days are also seen as extremely important events for the community. In 1964, St Peter's Italian Church in London was founded, and just a year later so too was the Church of Santa

Francesca Cabrini in Bedford - one of the very first Italian parish churches in Britain (Colpi 1991). In cultural terms, having their own church and events was essential for preserving the traditions of southern Italian Catholics. As a result, Santa Francesca immediately became the heart of all of the activities within the community. The priests were not only religious leaders but they also occupied the role of social workers. They founded a nursery, a youth club, and housed the first Italian welfare agency. From 1961 to the present day, and under the direction of the sisters of the House of Nazareth, the nursery has allowed Italian mothers to continue working in the knowledge that their children are being well looked after.

In the 1960s and 1970s, thanks again to the local churches in Bedford, another traditional Italian activity became available. Known as *doposcuola*, it provided a place for extracurricular activities for children: they were able to do their homework during *doposcuola* and an opportunity for language lessons after school or on Saturday mornings was also provided. These language lessons were of fundamental importance because most children within the community were able to speak only their parents' local dialect, and as a result, when they started school, communication became a problem. They had to learn English quickly, in order to communicate at school and outside the home and *doposcuola* also helped them to learn standard Italian. They found themselves in the position of being trilingual as a result, speaking their parents' hometown dialect as their mother tongue, while also acquiring Italian and English as a second and a third language.

As previously mentioned, not only were social events organized by the parish, but a large number of clubs also developed around the churches making them the most important point of reference for Italian communities in Britain. By the 1960's, the priests had founded the youth club, which represented an important meeting place for the boys[2] in the community. The peer groups that were formed there often challenged the authority of their families and for the first time, a generation gap emerged. Second generation teenagers who had been born and brought up in urban Britain were now posing problems for their first generation parents who realized it was not going to be an easy task imposing southern Italian village traditions on them. The girls were not as difficult to keep under check and had much less freedom than their male siblings. The youth club itself, although founded and run by priests, was off limits to the girls as it was never considered a suitable social venue for them.

---

[2] Only male Italians were allowed in Youth Clubs at that time.

Figure 1-1. The first Italian settlement in and around Alexandra Rd, Bedford, UK.

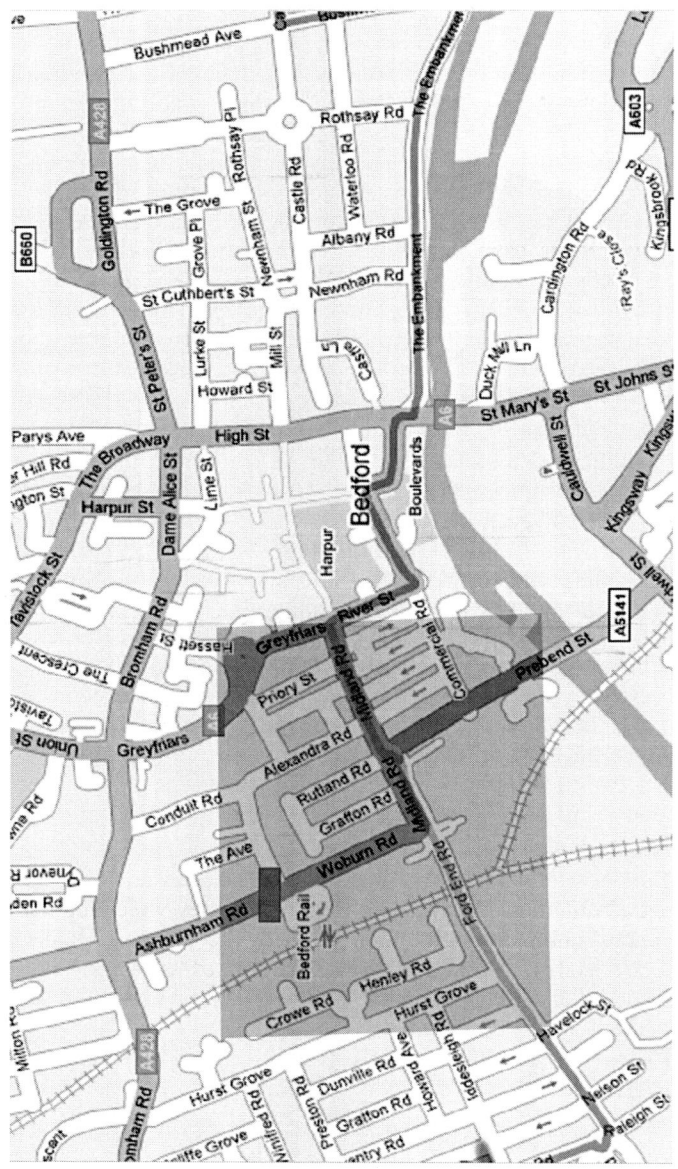

When the Italian Church of *Santa Francesca Cabrini* was built in Bedford, the priests organised a special celebration, or *festa*, in the large garden behind the church. The event, which was along traditional village lines, took place every year from the late 1960s onwards.

Football has always played an important social role for the community and in 1965, the Anglo Italian Football League was founded. It is still highly successful among the Italians of Bedford (Colpi 1991).

Last but not least, Bedford is the only non-capital city in the world to have had its own Italian vice-consulate. Having first opened in the town in 1954 to look after the needs of the many Italian settlers, it was closed in 2012 amid protests from the Italians inhabitants of Bedford and Italians from further afield.

1.2.3 Prosperity and development of work activities and political life

Throughout the 1970s, very little new migration was recorded from Italy to Britain, and for the first time the number of Italians returning to Italy exceeded the number of those migrating to the United Kingdom. At the same time, however, there was a new kind of short-term immigration involving Italian students who wanted to learn English as well as an influx of young people who came to the UK on working holidays. In 1973, Britain entered the European Community, and travelling to England became easier and mainly for pleasure, rather than a necessity.

The 1970s was a decade of integration and increasing prosperity for British Italians. The chain migration recruits of the 1950s and 1960s opened their own restaurants, sandwich bars, cafés, *pizzerias* and *trattorie*. As already mentioned strong family ties were extremely important for southern Italian communities, and not surprisingly, few marriages took place with people from outside the community. This strong sense of family and belonging persisted and loyalty to the community was a matter of pride. Most of the 1950s immigrants had purchased their own houses by this time and although still working long hours, they were frugal and able to save enough money to give their children the weddings that tradition demanded. Thanks to the churches which continued to be a focal point and the institutions, clubs, and associations that revolved around them, Italian traditions were preserved by the community.

In the 1980s, there was an interesting evolution in the make up of the Italian community in the UK. Firstly, there was an influx of educated Italians working in diplomatic positions, as well as Italian bankers and brokers, who were posted to Britain on a temporary basis. The

internationalionalization of banking and financial services, together with
the expansion of Italian diplomacy in Britain, gave rise to immigration of a
completely different type, adding another layer to the Italian community
and reflecting Italy's growing influence and prosperity (Colpi 1991).

Secondly, the number of associations that had formed within the
community increased significantly. With the encouragement of Italian
regional administrations, immigrants were brought together to create
associations like those of the *Trentini,* the *Campani* and the *Toscani,* for
example, based on the Italian regions or provinces they originated from.

Finally, throughout the decade there was an increase in political
activity in the Italian community. After the 1984 and 1989 European
Parliamentary Elections, it became legal for Italian residents in the UK to
vote for Italian candidates; a change which led to more participation in
Italian political affairs. Moreover, in 1989 internal community elections
were organised by Italian Consulates on behalf of the Italian government.
This important experiment allowed the community to select its own party
leaders. Thus, four consultative committees representing the areas of
London, Manchester, Edinburgh, and Bedford came into being, and twelve
members of each *Co.Em.It*[3]. were elected.

Despite the last decade of the 20th century being characterised by the
ever-increasing power of London as the most dominant focal point of
attraction for Italians in Britain, the large southern Italian post-World War
II communities still remain very active. They have consolidated their
position in Britain but never abandoned the Italian traditions they have
fought to maintain for decades and for generations. Thanks to their
economic success, Italian community members can often afford to have
two homes, one in Britain and one in Italy, and are able to spend time in
both countries feeling equally at home in either. Consequently, the idea of
"going home" at retirement age is no longer as compelling. This was in
fact the obsession of previous generations who were forced to scrimp and
save in the UK and live very modestly with the aim of investing in
property in Italy. It was very common for Italian immigrants to hope to
return to their towns and villages in their old age and to have a more
dignified life than the one they had left behind decades before.

---

[3] *Co.Em.It* stands for *Comitati dell'Emigrazione Italiana* (Committee on Italian
Migration). Law 205 8th May 1985.

1.3 Immigrants' language ability

Minority communities often struggle to fit in for a number of reasons. These can be social, cultural or religious but immigrants also struggle to integrate into the host community because of language barriers. Language acquisition has an important role to play in making integration smoother. Studies on language maintenance and shift amongst these communities have often focused on the level of linguistic competence displayed by immigrants. Language change and cultural assimilation within the same ethnic group and across host communities have been at the centre of many investigations. The following study on Italian immigrants in Australia can shed some light on the problems faced by Bedford Italians in England and their integration in the host community. A degree of mutual intelligibility between the immigrants and the society they live in is not always easy to achieve, since most of the time, the immigrants do not even speak the Standard language of their own country; they speak the dialect of their hometown as their first language and Italian as their second.

The different sociolinguistic situation of the country of origin has a great impact on intelligibility, (Tosi 1984) mainly for two reasons: firstly, although both Italian and its dialects derived from Latin and other Romance languages, over the centuries they have developed independent systems which are different in lexicon, grammar and phonology. Only in the last century have Standard Italian and its dialects started to produce a koineization that has given rise to a regionalization of Standard Italian. In the rural areas of Italy, however, where no regional koine has developed, speakers have shown significant levels of mutual unintelligibility with the dialects spoken in neighbouring villages or in other regions. Some unintelligibility was also clearly displayed towards Standard national Italian.

Secondly, and further to the above, among uneducated speakers, linguistic competence in the Standard language was at even lower levels. Not only did the process of koineization not affect them, but their knowledge of the Standard also depended more on the environmental exposure they might experience. Depending on the intensity of exposure, as well as on the geographical proximity to the national Standard, the speakers would develop gradual "transference skills" (Tosi 1984), improving their very poor language competence. On the contrary, where there was no contact with the Standard – as in the case of immigrants, for instance – their knowledge could slip back to the previous stage of unintelligibility and any communication with a speaker of the Standard would once again become very difficult. At times, this could lead to interference and hypercorrectness on the part of the speaker who attempts some form of communication, and he or she may end up sounding like a non-native speaker.

The dialectophone nature of Italian migrants as monolinguals has, however, been overemphasized at times and their knowledge of Italian underestimated. Confirming Bettoni and Gibbons (1988:16), Rubino (2002) claims that the Italians who arrived in Australia in the same period, the early 1950s, were highly sensitive to the prestige of Standard Italian. The same study agrees with De Mauro (1970) who states that migration favours the process of standardization since speakers of different dialects are brought into contact and almost forced to shift to the common ground of Standard Italian in order to be able to communicate.

Italian migration to Australia, as described by Rubino (2002), shares a great number of features with the migration of Italian settlers to Bedford. At the same time as learning English, children of both groups were growing up in close-knit communities where southern Italian dialects were spoken. Although mainly from small rural areas and the poorest regions of Italy, such as Sicily, Campania and Calabria, many other migrants also arrived from the northern region of Veneto. This wave was unlike the mass migration of Italians who arrived in Australia in the same decade 1951-1961 (Rubino 2002). In that case, a higher degree of accommodation was required because of their lack of proficiency in English. In order to reach an acceptable level of mutual intelligibility, the Italian migrants who went to Australia were more likely to converge on Standard Italian than the southern Italian migrants to Bedford.

1.3.1 First-generation immigrants' language origins

As in Tosi (1984), the language of Bedford immigrants is made up of the three main dialects which were spoken in the South of Italy at the time of their migration to the United Kingdom: the Molise dialect, the Campania-Irpinia dialect, and a southwestern variety of Sicilian. The three dialects differ in lexicon, grammar and phonology. They all belong to the southern Italian dialects that are mainly characterised by two types: Neapolitan and Sicilian. Within those two subdivisions, many other sub-dialects are to be found: different forms of the same dialects within the same province, the same town, and even the same village, especially in isolated and rural areas of Italy. Sometimes mutual intelligibility is not easy to achieve, and only in neighbouring dialects are the speakers more able to understand each other.

All migrants to Bedford primarily spoke village dialects as their mother tongue, and Standard Italian as their second language, but once in Britain, the host country, they had to acquire English as a foreign language. The vast majority of them, however, had received very little formal schooling. Those who had had the chance to complete primary school were male, while most of the female migrants never had the same opportunity. Most of these migrants were, therefore, almost illiterate, and their reading ability was only slightly better than that of their writing (Tosi 1984). In their villages there had been no real need for anything other than oral communication and they were all perfectly capable of fully understanding a Standard Italian speaker. Once these people moved to Britain however, their contact with the national language reduced dramatically and, as a result, they rarely improved their competence in Standard Italian. Again, their ability in the Standard has to be seen as related to their exposure to the language during adulthood (Tosi 1984), much more than to their years at school in formal education. Non-exposure in later life resulted in further linguistic impoverishment.

At the time of the migrants' departure for Britain, the position of women within the village differed greatly from that of the men. Looking at gender differences we see that only men were involved in the arena of public activities and it was in that arena that the use of the Standard was required. Men were in charge of dealing with bureaucracy and the authorities, such as the police, schools, public offices and so on. Any other kind of business outside the village, including military service, was the preserve of the men. On the contrary, since women typically lived with their families and with whom only dialect was spoken, they did not need any form of competence in standard Italian (Tosi 1984).

Not surprisingly, once they arrived in Britain and with so little schooling, learning English proved difficult for first generation Italians. Under pressure from the English-speaking world in which they were settling, the language they used was based mainly on improvisation and guesswork and often contained a set of lexical transferences, including the well-known examples of *il carro* and *la fenza* from the English *car* and *fence* (Rando 1968 as in Rubino 2000) which are examples of crosslinguistic blending.

1.3.2 The immigrants' language use and code-switching

The linguistic tool adopted for communication by Italian immigrants in Britain was the village dialect, and it was used at home with family, friends and all the other members of the community. Nonetheless, depending on the context, topic, situation, and interlocutor, first-generation speakers would mix and alternate their dialects with features of Standard Italian and/or English. As they learned new items due to everyday exposure, they added them to their linguistic repertoire.

Code-switching among Italians in Britain was of mainly three types: occasional switching, recurrent switching into Standard Italian, and recurrent switching into English (Tosi 1984).

An *occasional switching phenomenon* is encountered when single terms are learnt in an environment which is different from that of the family or the community, for instance during business or administrative operations with British and Italian institutions. On those occasions, speakers pick up terms which might be lacking in the repertoire of their dialect, and then reproduce them while talking to any other interlocutor who, depending on his or her own linguistic competence, might or might not fully understand. Usually, the terms which are more likely to show occasional switching phenomena are those which would otherwise have been unfamiliar to the immigrant, such as borrowed words from administrative or business vocabulary. Those borrowings do not imply the assimilation of ideas or feelings, and therefore cannot be indicated as marking a shift in the repertoire of the speaker. On the other hand, in daily conversations within the family or when interacting with other community members from the same village of origin, speakers make use of their dialect as the principal means of communication, given that topics are usually related to everyday life such as family events, children, and celebrations (Tosi 1984).

Recurrent switching into Standard Italian occurs when a conversation takes place between a community member and a newcomer, a temporary visitor, a new acquaintance, or an Italian from a different region to that of the speaker, as for instance in the case of northern Italians. This kind of code-switching above all, implies the use of standard forms of Italian. On such occasions, the subject combines the dialect of his or her village with features of Standard Italian. This may happen, for instance, in Consulate offices if no member of the staff comes from the same region as the speaker. Code-switching is an example of accommodating to the interlocutor in order to create a more comfortable linguistic environment for all speakers.

The last of the three types regards the relationship between first generation Italians and the English language. Whenever they came into contact with native speakers of English, Italians had to express themselves in the foreign language. These occasions were limited (Tosi 1984), and most *recurrent switching into English* happened in shops, offices, hospitals, schools and public administration offices. This variety could be called 'survival English' as it enabled Italians to develop short, practical conversations that could also be used in the working environment. For women who worked outside the home, competence was similar to that of the men. The older first-generation female immigrants, on the other hand, spent their lives mostly at home and ventured out only and almost exclusively when visiting relatives. As these opportunities were limited, they never learnt to speak English competently.

Even today, as the analysis carried out for the present investigation will reveal, first-generation competence in English is quite limited, mainly resulting in unsatisfactory usage due to an inadequate knowledge of Standard English grammar. There is also a strong presence of Italian-based structures, as well as heavily marked Italian-influenced phonology.

3 types of CS

CHAPTER TWO

METHODOLOGY:
THEORY AND PRACTICE

"All words have the 'taste' of a profession, a genre, a tendency, a party, a particular work, a particular person, a generation, an age group, the day and hour. Each word tastes of the context and contexts in which it has lived its socially changed life". (Bakhtin 1981:293)

2.1 Language, a Very Social Practice

According to Chambers (2004), three social categories are essential in sociolinguistic research: age, social class and sex. For Trudgill (2004), on the other hand, four categories contribute to variation: social context, social class, sex and gender, and ethnicity. A further structural variable for language variation is style (Coupland 2007), where the emphasis is on the context and confirms social influence on speech. Considering the many variables that exert an influence, sociolinguists have preferred the term "speech community" to that of "language", and more recently, have even more widely researched the idea of a "community of practice".

The notion of a "community of practice", as a model of social learning, understanding and development of how people interact in a specific setting, was first coined by Lave and Wenger (1991) and Wegner (1998), then reworked by Eckert (2000), Holmes and Mayerhoff (1999), Rampton (2000) focusing on the social "doing" more than on the structural "being". According to Eckert, the concept focuses more on the membership of a social group, on the ongoing co-construction of both an individual as well as a community identity. As in the quotation taken from Coupland (2007), Penelope Eckert clearly illustrates the model of a "community of practice" as follows:

"Meaning is made as people jointly construct relations through the development of a mutual view of, and in relation to, the communities and people around them. This meaning-making takes place in myriad contacts and associations both with and beyond dense social networks. To capture the process of meaning-making, we need to focus on a level of social organization at which individual and group identities are being constructed, and in which we can observe the emergence of symbolic processes that tie individuals to groups, and groups to the social context in which they gain meaning".

In her study of two groups of adolescents in the Detroit suburbs, the jocks and the burnouts, she analyses how style is represented in their speech as well as in their physical appearance, identifying and defining specific features that characterise the adolescents' speech. Social settings become central in the analysis of how people progressively change and construct their identities in social environments (2007). In Eckert's terms (2000 as in Coupland 2007), building on a theory of structure, the focus is on the contextual construction of social meaning, for which sociolinguistic variation can work out "meaning in relation to local contexts and issues" going beyond the variables of social class, age and ethnicity and including the new and more local social categories that can emerge. In the present study some parallels will be drawn with 3rd generation BIs and examples given of specific features that would seem to confirm how social settings, in this case the BIs' involvement with Punjabi, Pakistani and Caribbean minority groups, seem to influence 3rd generation BIs' speech.

2.2 Style and audience design approach

"Even if we are on our guard against the implication that the regions of language in which style resides are linguistically non-significant, we are still drawing the wrong line. There are no regions of language in which style does not reside". (Halliday 1996 [1965]: 63 as in Coupland 2007)

Halliday claims it is unrealistic to exclude style from the set. In Halliday's conception, style, or register, deals with the linguistic choices of a speaker driven by specific communicative purposes and circumstances. Speakers' choices in discourse reflect the social context, and in its general perspective on style, of dimensions of language organisation. Style is part of the communicative activity of speakers and part of the process of meaning-making in discourse systematic functional linguistics has helped sociolinguistics by above all emphasising the socio-semantically motivated aspect of style (Coupland 2007).

Going beyond Halliday, bearing in mind the concept of register as a way of speaking which is linked to situational genres defined by the speakers who are addressed (Coupland, Coupland and Giles 1991), and assuming that linear variables as well as linear principles are not enough to approach stylistic variation, two closely related models need to be introduced: *audience design* and *accommodation theory*.

The first approach is primarily associated with Allan Bell's research, the latter with Howard Giles and his colleagues' work, for which style variation can be explained in terms of how speakers design their speech in relation to their audience. Bell's study is of fundamental importance for the research carried out on Bedford Italians and the influence of the workplace on linguistic choices. Linguistic choices in terms of speaker-listener relationships were explained in previous approaches (Brown and Gilman 1960; Brown and Ford 1961; Ervin-Tripp 1973), and politeness research, inspired by Erving Goffman's work on the presentation of self in everyday life (Goffman 1959), also concentrated on the key aspects of social relationships and how discourse displays them (Brown and Levinson 1987). The label was of course not new either, it derived from Sacks, Schegloff and Jefferson's "recipient design" (1974) by way of Clark (Clark and Carlson 1982).

In 1984, Bell's research on broadcast news in New Zealand accounted for variation through what he elaborated as the *audience design* approach. In more recent times, in 2001 in fact, he revisited his own model and improved its weaker aspects. In his study, Bell, who had recorded several radio station broadcasts, focused on two stations in particular. Both stations' broadcasts came from the same studios and involved the same newsreaders. He compared their speech styles for the national station YA with the styles adopted for the community station ZB and looked for an explanation for the style-shift he had found in his doctoral research in 1977. Through a systematic analysis of a set of linguistics variables, he contrasted the two contexts of broadcasting, concluding that:

> "The newsreaders shifted on average 20 percent in each linguistic environment between stations YA and ZB. Single newsreaders heard on two different stations showed a consistent ability to make considerable style-shifts to suit the audience". (2001: 140)

According to Bell's interpretation, considering that at least four relevant dimensions, such as the speech genre (i.e. news reading), the speakers, the context, and the setting are constant for the two contexts under investigation, only the audience, in its being national versus local, changes and leads to a shift in style.

Guided by Hymes' multi-dimensional model of context (1972), Bell proposes a more elaborate version which suggests the main principles for style analysis when adopting an audience design framework. Quoting Bell 2001: 141-48, the main points are:

1. "Style is what an individual speaker does with a language in relation to other people."

The focus is on the individual, and style is essentially a social thing. In so saying, Bell marks the intra-speaker character as a consequence of inter-speaker variation.

2. "Style derives its meaning from the association of linguistic features with particular social groups."

As already noted by Ferguson and Gumpertz (2000 as in Bell 2001), Bell considers that social evaluation is transferred to the linguistic features associated with a specific group, for which the valuation of a linguistic variable and style-shift of that variable are mutual. Style is therefore associated with a particular group or situation, and based on associations.

3. "Speakers design their style primarily for and in response to their audience."

Bell says that "style shift occurs primarily in response to a change in the speaker's audience", and that is the core of his approach. Agreeing with the central idea within Giles' *accommodation theory*, there is a "convergence" for which a speaker shifts in style to be more like that of the person the speaker is talking to. According to these assumptions, style is actively responsive to the audience, also confirming Bakhtin's dialogical view of language, in accordance with which nothing is worse than a "lack of response" ([Bakhtin 1986:127] as in Bell 2001).

4. "Audience design applies to all codes and levels of a language repertoire, monolingual and multilingual."

Although Bell carried out a socio-phonetic analysis of his data, he claims that audience design does not refer only to style-shift but can be applied to other levels of linguistic variation, other languages, various repertoires within one speech community, including code-switching bilingual situations and monolingual style-shifts.

5.   "Variation on the style dimension within the speech of a style
      speaker derives from and echoes the variation which exists
      between speakers on the "social" dimension."

Unlike the previous principle, the fifth looks at style as a "dimension" of
variation which is separated from "social" variation. The Style Axiom (Bell
1984:151) claims that the same linguistic variables function simultaneously
on both social and stylistic levels, so that if one isolated feature or pattern is
used differently by speakers of different age or ethnicity, considering the
audience design as a strategy used by speakers to respond to different
audiences, "then it will be used differently to those people as listeners".

6.   "Speakers have a fine-grained ability to design their style for a
      range of different addressees, as well as for other audience
      members."

Again corresponding to the findings of the accommodation theory, the
speakers design their style according to a wide range of interlocutors, as
my own research on Bedford Italians will also show. Likewise, some more
fine-drawn patterns of co-variation in the speech of – in this case – both
speakers and listeners were demonstrated in Coupland's (1988, 2007)
work.

7.   "Style-shifting according to topic or setting derives its meaning
      and direction of style from the underlying association of topics
      and settings with typical audience members."

Interestingly, by this seventh principle Bell claims that although
strictly related to individual responses to their audience, whole social
situations can be explained according to the imprint they carry in different
settings or topics.

8.   "As well as the "responsive" dimension of style, there is the
      "initiative" dimension where the style-shift itself initiates a
      change in the situation rather than resulting from such a change."

Going beyond Blom and Gumperz's (1972) *situational* and
metaphorical switching distinctions, and above all their idea of
metaphorical code-switching, Bell suggests his idea of initiative style, for
which the audience design model is not only responsive to the type of
audience, but can also initiate a shift. The balancing of response and
initiation is one of the principles Bell reworked in 2001.

9.   "Initiative style-shifts are in essence "referee design" by which
      the linguistic features associated with a reference group can be
      used to express identification with that group."

Trying to link initiative style with what has been claimed so far, Bell
suggests the notion of "referee design", focusing on an absent reference
group. Referees, he argues, are third persons not often present at an
interaction but influencing the group even in their absence. For example,
referee design includes the adoption of a non-native accent or dialect by
native speakers of a different variety, as in Sue Fox's research about the
use of Bangladesh English by British youth, or Schilling-Estes' study
(1998) of the hyper-use of local dialect variants. In those cases, speakers
shift to identify with their ingroup or outgroup. Speakers identify with
potentially non-present groups.

10.   "Style research requires its own design and methodologies."

With this last principle, Bell calls for more recognition and progress
beyond the actual approach to style, which needs to be more central and
play a different role in research studies. He argues style should not be an
additional factor in studies with other main aims, it should "be tailored to
that end" and be investigated in its own right. (Bell 2001: 141-48)

2.3 Communication Accommodation Theory

First developed by Howard Giles in the 1970s (Giles 1973; Giles and
Powesland 1975) *as speech accommodation theory*, then renamed
communication accommodation theory, this is an alternative explanation
for stylistic variation as described by Labov, alongside Allan Bell's
audience design.

Focusing on the motivational aspects for which speakers modify their
speech, a speaker can *converge* or *diverge* his or her speech in accordance
with that of a listener, in an attempt to either seek social approval or
communication efficiency (Coupland 2007). The accommodation model
relates to all communicative features and styles, underlying the degree of
similarity or difference between speakers and listeners. Genessee and
Bourhis ([1988] as in Coupland 2007), for instance, showed how contextual
understanding can sometimes impede accommodation. In their study they
illustrate how a salesperson converging with the communicative styles of
customers does not increase his or her social attractiveness. As a result,
being aware of the social norms governing commercial sales, customers

predict and understand the strategies behind a salesman's accommodation and therefore form predetermined expectations.

Based on the accommodation model characteristics, it is very often applied along with the audience design approach as in the present study.

2.4 Limits of audience-focused perspectives

Audience design and accommodation theory are the core concepts characterising the study of style in the 1980s and 1990s among variationist sociolinguists (Coupland 2007). Their applications brought valuable results; nonetheless, audience-focused perspectives also showed some limitations and critiques.

One of the critiques maintains that there is a large use of quantitative patterns. Excessive systematization of style can be seen as reductionism, minimising the complexity of speakers' use of language. The measured levels of "social" variation cannot overcome the problem regarding which speakers appear in the sample under investigation and how they are surveyed. It is extremely difficult to believe that we can embody maximal levels of sociolinguistic variation in a community. It is worth pointing out that although Bell is clearly right in saying, "Speakers cannot match the speech differences of all their interlocutors" (Bell 1984), the comparison of "social" and "stylistic" variation levels do not sometimes appear to be adequately motivated.

On the other hand, saying that social categories do not fully determine speech style can also be seen as one of the greatest achievements of the audience design and accommodation model. They show how flexible and multifaceted sociolinguistic identity can be, although apparently limited by fixed categories (Coupland 2007). Both models allow a degree of convergence or divergence in speakers' speech, which modifies their stylistic selections according to situations and addressees. Moreover, as Bell (2001) argues, individual speakers use style, as well as other aspects of their repertoire, to represent their identity.

The problem, conversely, could lie in the concept of *audience*: has it been fully theorised and described? Audience types bring us back to Goffman's descriptions (1981) of "Addressee", "Auditor", "Overhearer", and "Eavesdropper". All but "eavesdroppers" are directly addressed types of audience[4]. Based on Goffman's distinctions of addressed types, Bell (1984) suggests that there are degrees and grades according to the distance

---

[4] Although as in the case of 'Overhearers', they are like "Auditors" despite non being ratified, i.e. the speakers are not aware of their presence and are not intended recipients of speech. (Coupland 2007)

from the speaker. In other words, according to the distance and the audience role, there is less of an "effect" or an "influence" on a speaker's style.

Yet the role of "audienceship" still requires further theorisation. Are we all dealing with "audienceship" in the same way? If we take for instance the case of Bell's research about radio announcers and we discuss the type of audience as the main parameter, we can consider their audience only in an abstract sense, which was clearly present only in the minds of the announcers. Alternatively, let us consider Coupland's case study of a travel agency in Cardiff (1980, 2007). The service setting offered the possibility of including a variety of social classes, ages and so on, representing a useful site for investigation. In the course of the research, Coupland became interested in the speech of agency assistants, female workers, who provided the service to different customers everyday, both through face-to-face and telephone interactions; giving advice, making bookings, taking payments, and so on. Coupland (1980, 1988) concentrated on one assistant, Sue, who produced three different "levels of standardness" across different contexts, shifting according to participants. Customers were predominantly unfamiliar to her, yet Sue tried to establish a degree of stylistic convergence, or closeness, during the encounters as part of her job. Those two cases are examples of style studies through different relational models, in which social relation is negotiated differently. In the first case, for instance, we have an example of how style can be referred to an ideal rather than the actual recipient (Bell 1984), so again, "audienceship" is central to the discussion. We should question what is implied in the idea of "style for audience", since it can appear to be similar to "style in response to their audience", which is not exactly the case. According to Coupland (2007:78), although they can be parallel,

" 'Style for audience' represents speakers' actions as being active and agentive. 'Style in response to an audience' paints speaker actions as being more passive and automated (although Bell says not)".

In Bell's response he insists on saying that there is strategic action in the "audience design", assuming there is no distinction between active and passive responsiveness in this case. Dealing with each other, signalling some style convergence represents a response to one another which is not passive manipulation, although he says "people do, after all, generally spend more time responding to others than taking the initiative" (Bell 1984:184). Despite various attempts to clarify these aspects of both approaches, the relativity of speaker responsiveness as well as of "audienceship" remains unclear. What is interesting to note is that the strength of audience design, as proposed by Bell in 1984, is in its fallibility, for which the predictions can also be proved wrong. The explanations as to why a speaker chose to say something a certain way on a specific occasion may go beyond accommodation to the audience, but what is certainly going on in talk design is in relation to addressees in a way that is an extension of the audience approach.

Speaker motivations are crucial to both models and seeking the "addressees' approval" (Bell 1984) represents one common factor. Speakers design their talk for their audience according to Bell, as well as designing it in relation to their "referee groups". A speaker converges in order to be perceived as socially appealing, bringing back the main questions for stylistic variation: "*Who, actually, is style for?*" (Coupland 2007). If "seeking approval" is unquestionably a central concept, the other claim for which convergence is actually a way to be "communicatively effective" is not as unambiguous. It seems restrictive to set priorities in favour of speakers or listeners, whether they be targets or beneficiaries of the stylistic process.

To conclude, as Bell argues (2001:164 my emphasis), "*a part* of our behaviour is a reflection of the social characteristics of groups we are associated with", although labels and categories may change in different situations or according to different groups.

2.5 Workplace encounters

Traditionally, participants in workplace encounters concentrate primarily on the accomplishment of specific workplace tasks, and therefore on transactional goals. Although commonly considered to be a type of institutional discourse, and distinct from ordinary conversation as it involves an "orientation by at least one of the participants to some core goal, task or identity ... conventionally associated with the institution" (Drew and Heritage 1992:22), workplace talk is not always task-focused (Koester 2004) but can also concern relational interests. Lampi (1986) also draws a distinction when analysing business negotiations. She distinguishes between "task-orientation", "interaction-orientation" and "self-orientation". "Identity goals", on the other hand, as based on the Ylänne-McEwen analysis of interactions in travel agencies (1996), can be linked to both transactional and relational orientation, as speakers can make either institutional roles or identities salient in terms of relational goals.

On the other hand, in some types of workplace discourse, speakers may be essentially interested in getting things done, therefore concerned with transactional goals, as in the case of service encounters between strangers (Drew and Heritage 1992), probably because there is no need to maintain a relationship. However, research has shown the importance of relational goals in transactional situations, as in the CA studies concerning travel agencies (Coupland and Ylänne-McEwen 2000), telephone companies (Ragan 2000) or health care (Holmes and Stubbe 2003). It is not always easy to determine exactly what kind of activity the speakers are engaged in (Koester 2006). Sometimes the topics are unrelated to any workplace concerns and may resemble those of "small talk" rather than task-related discourses relating to completing activities at work.

Assuming Swales' definition of genre (1990: 58) as "a class of communicative events, the members of which share some set of communicative purposes", and in addition considering speech genre as having a sequential organisation, most studies have concentrated on the structure of service encounters. Hasan (1985) shows the importance of "obligatory elements" and "optional elements" in service encounters; other research suggests that the model is more complex (Ventola 1987, Mitchell 1975, Bakthin 1986). Most studies on service encounters focus mainly on transactional goals as for instance Mitchell's and Hasan's, but during service transactions, customers and servers may also engage in small talk. Some transactional genres do involve non-transactional talk, as for instance in McCarthy (2000) who found that less than 10% of conversations between hairdressers and their customers were task-focused.

Combining a genre approach to spoken discourse with a conversation analytic method, Koester (2004) provided interesting insights concerning relational talks within transactional workplace genres. He recorded three types of offices: university offices, editorial offices of a publishing company and companies in the private sector outside publishing, and although in most of the conversations he analysed, co-workers were engaging in a variety of tasks such as making arrangements, decision-making, request and favour-seeking, giving instructions and reporting, he also examined non-transactional conversations, referred to as "office gossip" or "small talk". Rather than performing workplace tasks, the participants were involved in other conversations which did not deal with workplace topics or tasks, but with informal chats about their private life, family, health, the weekend and so on. Confirming other recent research concerning workplace discourse (e.g., Holmes and Stubbe 2003, and Ragan 2000), Koester's analysis showed that participants in workplace encounters simultaneously pursue both transactional and relational goals, for which no clear distinction between institutional talk and ordinary conversation can be made. He therefore concludes by suggesting that "relational talk" is crucial within workplace discourse; and although it is difficult to establish systematic association between the workplace genre and relational talk, Koester claims that tendencies can be observed. Relational sequences, for instance, are more likely to occur in making arrangements, or while expressing appreciative remarks in procedural and requesting discourse. In his CA study, Koester therefore found some regularities but the workplace genre calls for further research in other directions as well. As Koester (2004, 2006) claims, genre analysis is useful in identifying recurrent structures across different instances of similar types of activities, whereas CA focuses more on "the turn-by-turn dynamics of talks as it develops". The present research, on the other hand, attempts to deal with workplace encounters by adopting a variationist approach and analysing a set of variables within an audience design model.

2.6 Methods

Effective communication with customers and colleagues is clearly crucial to the smooth and productive running of a business, but there is remarkably little research which examines in detail how immigrants verbally communicate in professional settings. The aim of this investigation is to present a sociolinguistic study of the ethnic minority community of Italians in Bedford, UK, to verify whether their local cultural heritage and linguistic identity are likely to find expression and reflection in the language they use in the workplace. Earlier work (Guzzo 2005, 2007), demonstrated a degree of language shift towards English as far as second and third generation Bedfordians of Italian origin were concerned, but nevertheless showed the maintenance of a strong Italian identity, and among the third generation Bedford Italians (BIs), whose L1 is English, a distinctively ethnically marked variety was detected. The present research specifically addresses ESP concerns, from the perspective of cross- and intra-cultural communication within a multicultural English city, such as Bedford. In order to explore the language of Italians at work, the investigation of the corpus has been carried out following two main methods: 1) an ethnographic approach as applied by sociolinguists to the study of language (Blom & Gumperz 1972, Milroy 1987, and Wei 1994) for which the methodology is based on a combination of participant observation and ethnographic data collection through the means of audio recordings, and 2) two related approaches of accommodation theory (Giles 1973, Giles and Powesland 1975) and audience design, as a confirmation of Bell's (1984, 2001) model.

2.6.1 Participant Observation

Participant observation is a key concept which usually requires an extended period of time in which the researcher actively takes part in the life of the community under scrutiny. It is a straightforward technique thanks to which the researcher is likely to gain a deeper understanding than would normally be possible when using questionnaire surveys alone. Participant observation is the principal research technique of ethnography, and although ethnography is primarily the study of culture developed by cultural anthropologists, the participant observation methods of ethnography have long been used in qualitative sociolinguistic research, and are also considered to be increasingly important in quantitative work (Agar 1996, Johnstone 2000, Milroy and Gordon 2003).

There have been many arguments in favour of this method through which it is possible to collect first-hand information or data. As Agar (1996:31) properly describes it, participant observation is the only way to access the community under investigation, by "establishing relationships with people, participating with them in what they do, and observing what is going on".

Discussions on sociolinguistic methods and data collection have often concentrated on the contrast between the use of prefabricated linguistic data and the use of observed naturally-occurring data. It is conventionally assumed that through *observation*, surveys and real spoken data analyses, it is possible to predict regularities and real patterns of language variation. In addition, one important step is to achieve neutral observation, objective quantitative analysis whose procedure needs to be repeatable, and minimise observer-effects. As outlined by William Labov (1972), the "observer's paradox" is a very important issue which arises during sociolinguistic research and needs to be minimised. The investigator aims to observe how people speak when they are not being observed, but the presence of the observer is very likely to distort, and sometimes even spoil, the object of observation, amd may interfere with naturalness. The concept of "good data" calls for necessary characteristics, such as the spontaneity of the data, their authenticity and representativeness, as well as requiring the use of high quality audio-recording. Although the presence of a fieldworker is almost certain to interfere with the naturalness of the informant's choice of words or his or her pronunciation (cf. Milroy and Gordon 2003), observation remains crucial for variationist studies. Fieldworkers have to keep in mind that the paradox can never be entirely resolved; nonetheless, entering the community can help to alleviate this phenomenon (Feagin 2004).

Sociolinguistic methods have also encompassed specific approaches to the community. In order to gain deeper ethnographic understanding, the primary resource is the researcher's understanding of the linguistic norms and contexts, something which is difficult to achieve from outside the community. The contexts in which the fieldworker operates and the behaviour of people are never stable. The interpretation of the interlocutor, and the studies that researchers conduct or the results they achieve, are never unquestionable. Participant observers spend time developing roles for themselves in the community in which they are interested. The more time they spend engaged in everyday tasks as an insider, such as talking, eating, working and living with the people they are studying, the easier it is to come to understand what is actually going on within the community.This helps to understand any rules that the community may have and the fieldworker becomes an "internal eye" and almost a member of the group itself (Milroy and Gordon, 2003).

2.6.2 The researcher's role

When approaching research using ethnographic techniques, one very important step is to gain access to the community. Once this is achieved, another factor which may affect the fieldwork needs to be taken into account: the linguistic background of the researcher. In the literature, very little has been documented concerning the language competence and background of the fieldworker. It is generally assumed that if the fieldworker shares some similar linguistic background with the interlocutor this can be helpful; the relationship is very likely to be established more quickly and can positively contribute to the development of the research (Wei 1994). Moreover, elements of non-standard forms of a language would be more likely to be revealed to a native speaker of the same variety (Trudgill 1974). Nonetheless, the majority of sociolinguistic studies tend to be carried out by non-native speakers as only a limited number of researchers can claim to have a close to native competence in the language or dialect spoken by the informant under analysis.

The fact that I was a Southern Italian represented a clear advantage; my own dialect competence has some relation to the village dialects spoken by the BIC members, and the ability to speak a dialect form similar to that of my interlocutors was an asset where fieldwork was concerned.

2.6.3 Ethics

Ethical issues have been widely discussed in the literature. Milroy (1987), Wei (1994), and Matsumoto (2001), to cite some, have expressed the importance of ethical behaviour during and after the development of the sociolinguistic study. The choice is between bluntly admitting that one is carrying out research, or being silent and not informing others that research is taking place. These two methods are respectively known as "overt" and "covert" (Jorgersen 1989 as in Wei 1994). In the case of an "overt method", researchers would accurately explain the type of study they are carrying out, pointing out their objectives and asking for authorisation. On the other hand, in the case of a "covert method", researchers would not be explicit about the study and the speaker would never be aware of being the object of analysis. Milroy (1987), for instance, adopts a "semi-covert method" in her study in Belfast. She informed most of her informants the research was taking place and shared details about the study, but never said explicitly what the object of her investigation was.

For the present study an "overt method" was adopted and the purposes of the research were explained. I was not new to the Bedford community as many of its members had already met me when I had spent a long period there in 2004 and had participated in community life. In recent years, I had always kept in touch with the friends I had made while living there and going back was a good opportunity to visit the many friends who perceive me as "one of them".

As a result, a very simple explanation of the present investigation was that it would be focussing on workplace language, and aiming to verifying whether some reflection of their Italian heritage existed in the type of language they spoke at work. The reaction to this information was positive and the informants showed an interest in the project expressing willingness to take part and to help in any way possible. They provided answers to questions and I was introduced to their social network of friends and colleagues, who on occasion spontaneously offered to be recorded. Thanks to the information provided, the informants seemed perfectly comfortable and extremely willing to contribute to a new study. Generally speaking, 1st and 2nd generation Italians complained there was usually too little outside interest in their community.

Anonymity was ensured and pseudonyms were used in the transcriptions. Each informant was given only a first name in the course of this research, as adopted in the corpus transcription. Great care was taken to ensure that mini disc recordings were kept private and alphanumeric codes were used to ensure anonymity. Access to the original recordings is restricted and available only to scholars other than myself for research purposes. As for the written questionnaires compiled for an earlier research project and used as background reference to the present investigation, all information provided is kept strictly confidential and will never be used for purposes other than academic research.

2.7 Corpus Construction

2.7.1 Corpus

As Britain claims (2007), most of the studies carried out to date have provided more quantitative analyses of phonological rather than grammatical variations in British English. Phonological studies have extensively investigated sound variation, and collections of larger corpora have helped systematic analyses in the field of morphology. Nonetheless, very little has been said about Italian immigrants in the United Kingdom with reference to their phonology or morphology in the context of the workplace.

As Scotton (1986) suggests, to carry out the analysis of individual language behaviour, an informant's verbal acts need to be contextualised within an analysis of the norms ruling the speech community in which the individuals live. In order to do so, this chapter presents the corpus, examining the language behaviour of members across three generations. 1st, 2nd, and 3rd generation Bedford Italians were studied focusing primarily on the speakers' choices of language style with different interlocutors in three specific workplace contexts. On the basis of this discussion, two phonological and three morphological variables are analysed and discussed according to the linguistic behaviour they display.

2.7.2 Corpus Selection

The data in this chapter are drawn from long-term participant observations in a range of three specific workplace situations. All linguistic variables under analysis have been detected in code switched contexts, while informants were either interacting with colleagues or customers. The ethnographic recordings took place in 11 workplaces which have been divided into three main subcategories: *seilers* (including wholesalers, retailers, and market traders), *restaurants* (including restaurants, pizzerias, kiosks, and take-aways), and *hairdressers* (including barber shops and salons). Findings are presented in the form of tables and figures showing results for each of the three generations in each of the three work subcategories, according to whether informants are speaking to Italian or British interlocutors. Following Bell's (1984, 2001) audience design model, and focusing on speakers' language choices in response to different interlocutors, intra-speaker and inter-speaker variations in language choice by speakers from three generations are examined and discussed in the present work.

In selecting informants, a network paradigm was applied to the present study. In Boissevain terms (1987: 169):

> "It [the social network analysis] asks questions about who is linked to whom, the nature of that linkage, and how the nature of the linkage effects behaviour".

Adopting this approach, all the informants were selected on the basis of their membership of the BIC and are connected to each other through kinship, friendship, or community acquaintanceship. Through the "friend of a friend" technique based on Milroy (1987) and Eckert (2000), I was introduced to a number of community members and by actively participating in the life of the community during my stay in town, I was able to carry out the fieldwork research.

2.7.3 Data Collection

The diversity that characterises social networks can represent a problem for the investigator. Methods of collecting data for network analysis can be of different types; some fieldworkers prefer to make use of self-reports, name-elicitations, observation of social interactions which are perhaps the most frequently used techniques for collecting data about personal networks, and then contrast them with other comparable information. Fischer (1982) proposes an example of interview question structure:

> "Some people never talk with anyone, either on or off the job, about how to do their work. Other people do discuss things like decisions they have to make, work problems they have to solve, and ways to do their work better. Is there anyone you talk with about how to do your work? [If yes] Who do you talk with about your work?" (Fischer, 1982: 324)

In my opinion, Fisher's suggestions for structuring an interview would result in a lack of naturalness and spontaneity as there would be a rigidly structured question-answer exchange rather than an informal interview.

On the other hand, according to Mitchell (1986 as in Wei 1994), by combining ethnographic interviews with participant observation, the investigator can examine networks better overall.

In the present study, the basis for examining the language behaviour of BIs at work, was to avoid question-answer techniques, self-reports, and interviews which would limit the spontaneity and truthfulness of the collected data. As previously mentioned, a combination of participant observation and ethnographic data collection through the means of audio recordings was opted for. Between April and September 2006, a total number of approximately 20 hours of spontaneous, naturally occurring workplace interactions in a range of 11 Bedford Italian workplaces were tape-recorded. The data include both face-to-face interactions and telephone calls, male and female workers, and both Bedford Italians and their British colleagues and/or customers. The social variable of gender was disregarded as far as the present analysis is concerned, whereas the variables of age (as expressed in the form of three generations of BI informants), ethnicity, geographical position, and occupation were the basis of the selection criteria.

In all the sites where data were collected, the methodology was designed to give participants maximum control over the data collection process in order not to interfere with their work. Moreover, those involved provided information on their ethnic background, home language, and age, as well as contextual information. They also gave permission for the data to be used for linguistic analysis and academic purposes. As for the informants' emigration background and duration of residence in the UK, all speakers belong to the BIC. First generation BIs either came to town with the first bulk of immigrants in the 1950s or with the second wave which lasted up until the end of the 1960s. All second and third generation informants were born and brought up in Bedford. Speakers whose BIC membership was questionable, were excluded from the analysis. For this reason, speakers who had only recently immigrated or belonged to neither the first nor second wave of migration of the BIC who settled in town, as well as those who spent most of their lives in Italy, were left out of the present analysis.

Once the 20-hour spoken corpus was completed, all files were digitised, cleaned and then burnt on to a DVD in order to improve the sound quality and reduce the level of noise. The long process of data transcription of all the audio recordings started at this stage. Once transcribed, my corpus consisted of about 65.000 words.

The corpus was transcribed using conventionalised IPA symbols as required. No use of Conversation Analysis procedures was necessary as far as the phonological and morphological analyses were concerned.

2.8 Audio Recordings

2.8.1 Tape-Recordings of Workplace Conversations

All the main approaches were used to collect the data in an attempt to reduce the inevitable "interference" effect of the researcher over the "naturalness" of the data, as discussed above. For the recordings, digital techniques were preferred, and a SONY MD Net MD Walkman MZ-N10 minidisk recorder combined with a SONY ECM-710 compact high performance stereo electret condenser microphone was used. A high-fidelity digital electronic recording machine, capable of recording the entire interaction for subsequent transcription and study was essential. Because the focus of the linguistic analysis was primarily on phonological and morphological behaviour, a digital recording technique was fundamental if the best possible audio was to be obtained.

To ensure that the data were natural and the workplace conversations spontaneous, informants were recorded while carrying out their normal work activities. As discussed in the previous chapter, one of the main concerns of fieldworkers is to ensure that the linguistic data faithfully represents the speakers' natural language behaviour (Hymes, 1974; Gumperz, 1982; Labov, 1966, 1972). The presence of interlocutors (including the addressee and hearer) could well be of critical importance when dealing with the naturalness of language in situational contexts (Wei, 1994; Bell, 1984). In this study, the presence of the researcher and the recorder was found to be intrusive for the first ten or fifteen minutes. To reduce the prominence of the investigator, avoid interference and achieve spontaneous language, a specific pattern was followed while informants were being recorded. Once permission to record had been given, the minidisk was placed where it would not interfere with the informants' normal work activities. The minidisk had to be positioned close enough to catch their voices, but not too close to distract them from their work. At times – as in the case of one hairdresser, for instance – informants requested and were granted a pinned microphone that would allow them to move around freely during recording. In most cases, after positioning the recording machine, informants were left alone to allow them to work and to interact normally without the pressure of the interviewer being present, and I returned only to stop the recording after

80 minutes had lapsed. In other instances, as in the recording labelled BED01, for example, due to my familiarity with some community members, my presence was considered in no way intimidating and as a result, interactions were natural and spontaneous.

2.8.2 Encoding results

Several attempts to systematise the methods of transcription, encoding and analysis of bilingual speakers in any language have been experimented. Li Wei (1994) adopted three language categories, such as C for Chinese, E for English, and CE when using both codes. On the other hand, Reynolds and Akram (1999), opted for four categories: i.e. Punjabi/Urdu monolingual, Punjabi/Urdu dominant bilingual, English dominant bilingual, English monolingual/passive bilingual. In many multilingual communities, however, language distinctions are not so neat (Matsumoto, 2002) as speakers tend to use a mixture of all languages they know, to different degrees.

In the present study, taking into account the linguistic variables under investigation and the aims of the research, conventionalised encoding methods were preferred. Adopting a standardised approach, each of the tape recordings was labelled using a code for the locality, indicating the place where the recording took place, a progressive number of recording, (e.g. BED01), and the date it was recorded (e.g. 11.04.2006).

2.9 Entering the Community

Traditionally, it is acknowledged that participant observers enter the community they aim at researching, and live within it: eating, working, and interacting with the community members they are studying. The research questions formulated, and the hypotheses for answering those questions vary notably when it comes to participant observation and studying a community. "Community", as Wei (1994) states, is a sociological concept which can be defined as "a cohesive and self-conscious social group" (Watson, 1977: 195, as in Wei 1994: 50). For this reason, choosing a community as a subject of analysis is a very protracted process with no specific time-frame. Moreover, exhaustive planning is impossible as each and every finding can open doors to more investigation, and the research questions posed at the beginning of the period of observation might have to be refined over and over again according to those findings (Spradley 1980 in Wei 1994).

In keeping with the ethnographic technique of participant observation, research for this study was initiated without a definite idea of the direction it would take as there were no specific samples or hypotheses to be verified. The main aim was to investigate the community of Bedford Italians following on from previous research which required further investigation.

It is worth noting that one of the main disadvantages of the participant observation method is the amount of time needed. Ethnographic approaches, as previously mentioned, are extremely time-consuming: they require months, if not years spent within the community of speakers, so as to be fully accepted as a member and to obtain a thorough knowledge of all its mechanisms, internal rules, social networks, and so forth. Although time was relatively limited in this particular case, the research led to very interesting results.

My first encounter with the BIC (Guzzo 2005), was made possible thanks to the Italian General Consulate in London, and the Italian Vice Consulate in Bedford. A number of visits to the town allowed details about the Italian inhabitants, their businesses, and their relationship with their motherland to be collected. After an adequate amount of general information had been acquired about the life of Italians in Bedford, an appointment was made to meet with the owner of one of the most well-known kiosks in town, Liberato Leonetti. This encounter with a community leader proved to be a real turning-point and allowed actual participation in the community. Liberato's parents migrated to Bedford in the early 1950s as did most of the Italians that came to work in the brick factories. He is a middle-aged, second generation Bedford Italian and owner of the kiosk *"La Piazza"*, an Italian-style kiosk located in the town centre which is a popular meeting place for many of the community members. He grew up in Bedford and, like most Italians, travels to Italy only on vacation. His cultural heritage is extremely strong and his patriotism very marked. From the first steps taken in the community, Liberato and his staff became precious for my fieldwork: they assisted me, gave me helpful advice and introduced me to other community members (Guzzo 2005).

2.9.1 Informants

Continued contact with the BI inhabitants I met in 2004 led to a strengthening of ties, and when I returned in 2006 to collect new data, the "friend of a friend" informal network technique based on Milroy (1987), and Eckert (2000) was adopted. Informants were introduced to me by other BI friends. Nonetheless, this was not always an advantage as some of the businesses I contacted for my investigation refused to be recorded. My final sample consists of a total of 11 businesses run by community members, grouped into three main subcategories: *restaurants* (including restaurants, pizzerias, kiosks, and take-aways), *sellers* (including wholesalers, retailers, and market traders), and *hairdressers* (including barber shops and hairdressers). The overall number of informants recorded and analysed consists of 100 BIs. The total number includes both employers and employees of the businesses who authorised the recordings, as well as the BI customers who took part in the business interactions.

The category labelled *restaurants* includes restaurants, pizzerias, kiosks, and take-aways and refers to the following recordings: BED01 the kiosk "La Piazza"[5], BED02 the restaurant "Cappuccino Bar", BED05 the take-away pizzeria "Chirico's", BED06 the restaurant "La Dolce Vita", and BED10 the restaurant pizzeria "Santaniello's". The second workplace setting was categorized as *sellers* and includes wholesalers, retailers, and market traders. This subdivision refers to the recordings encoded BED03 and BED04 (grouped in one single entity because both recordings referred to the same market trader) which took place at the market stall "Chirico's", BED07 the wholesaler "AB Fruit", and BED08 the bakery offering catering services named "La Rondine". Finally, as for the third and last category of workplaces, labelled *hairdressers*, this includes barber shops and salons. This category refers to the recording BED09 the barber shop "Tony's", BED11 the ladies and gents hairdresser "Vincenzo's", and BED12 the hairdresser/barber shop "Giovanni's".

More specifically, as for the first dataset recorded, a short description of the informants in the *restaurants* data category follows. Let us start with the above mentioned BED01 "La Piazza", an Italian-style kiosk which is situated in the town centre. The owner Liberato Leonetti, a 2nd generation 42-year-old BI male, and his staff offer genuine Italian food and drinks which are highly appreciated by their customers who regularly stop for a *cappuccino* in the morning, a *panino*, or a *pasta dish* at lunch time. The type of customers represents a miscellaneous group where BIs predominate over the British or other minority ethnic groups. A very friendly, relaxed atmosphere welcomes customers who tend to visit more than once a day to buy food and beverages and also to spend time with their friends.

---

[5] Please note that anonymity was ensured for all informants and pseudonyms were used in the transcriptions. Each informant was given only a first name or initial(s) in the course of this research.

BED02 "Cappuccino Bar" is owned by the BI Spiniello family. Federico, the owner, is a 2nd generation BI male in his late fifties who is married to a 2nd generation BI female. He runs a small Italian restaurant in the town centre. with his children and employees who are BI or British. The first part of the recording took place in the restaurant kitchen where Federico and his nephew, Gerardo[6], were preparing food, while the second part took place at the bar.

BED05 "Chirico's" is one of several businesses owned by the Chirico family, one of the oldest Italian families in town. Mrs Sandra Chirico is a 2nd generation BI female in her fifties, who was born and brought up in Bedford by Italian parents who migrated with the very first flow of immigrants at the beginning of the 1950s with the intention of working in the brick factories. Her family was originally from the area of Caserta, and nowadays, most of its members who moved to Bedford work in the catering business. At the take-away pizzeria 'Chirico's', Mrs Chirico works mainly with her son Enrico, a 3rd generation 34-year-old, and Anna, her younger niece. The friendly atmosphere at the take-away pizza house attracts many Bedfordians thanks to its large variety of home-made Italian-style pizzas.

BED06 "La Dolce Vita" is an elegant Italian restaurant owned by another member of the Chirico family, Domenico Sacco, who is Mrs Chirico's cousin, and a 2nd generation 47-year-old BI. The bistro is atypical, and serves finer food than most restaurants in Bedford. The refined atmosphere is enhanced by playing both Italian and international music in the background. Customers are mainly British males and females but there are fewer BIs.

BED10 "Santaniello's", on the other hand, is a very typical Italian pizza restaurant. Gerardo Santaniello is a 2nd generation, 55-year-old male who owns and manages the pizzeria with his son Fiorangelo and many BI employees. The pizza maker is a 1st generation BI who arrived in the town in the late 1960s with the last flow of Italian immigrants. The pizza house boasts one of the very rare wood-burning ovens in the UK, and the expertise of the pizza maker, Antonio, is put on show during what can be considered first-rate performances in traditional Neapolitan pizza-making. The restaurant is welcoming, always very crowded, and especially hectic at dinner time. The number of waiters and waitresses, mainly 3rd generation BIs, varies at different times of the week. Although most of the

---

[6] Please note that Gerardo, one of the speakers mentioned, was born and brought up in Italy, and has spent most of his life there. He is a relative of the Spiniello family who still live in Italy. He has only recently emigrated to Bedford and was not included in the present analysis.

customers are BI members, other pizza connoisseurs join them quite regularly.

As for the second set of businesses, *sellers*, BED03-BED04 refers to the market stall "Chirico's". The market trader is Mrs Maria Chirico, Sandra's sister. She works at the market twice a week, selling the bread made at Chirico's bakery. Her son, Roberto and her daughters, Anna and Deborah, often help her out. Her stall is one of the most popular at the market, and although her customers are mainly British, many BIs make a point of going there to buy her fresh bread. The BIs who go to the market are predominantly 1st generation and interestingly, during these market encounters, the language of communication is exclusively Italian[7].

BED07 "AB Fruits" is a wholesale company which supplies foodstuffs to restaurants and shops. It belongs to the Bosco family, one of the largest in town, and the business is managed by two brothers, Angelo and Sabino Bosco. They are both 2nd generation BIs, and it is worth noting that only BIs and newly-arrived Italian employees are employed in an attempt to maintain the Italianness of the group and also to avoid having 'outsiders' amongst their staff. Their customers are quite mixed. The recording took place in one of the offices, and telephone calls were included in the analysis.

BED08 "La Rondine" is a confectionery manufacturing company that also deals with banqueting services. The company is run by the Garganese family: Salvatore, aged 55, and his sister Elisabetta, aged 58. They are 2nd generation BIs whose parents emigrated from Apulia in the early 1950s to work for the Bedfordshire brick companies. The confectionery is a well-equipped laboratory, where cakes and pastries are produced. Their employees are mainly BIs, whereas their customers are mixed. The company offers wedding and party banqueting and represents one of the most popular catering services amongst BI members.

Lastly, the third dataset of workplaces recorded for the present study is labelled *hairdressers*, including barber shops, and ladies' and gents' salons. BED09 "Tony's" barber shop is one of the oldest in town. The owner, Antonio De Piano, in his late sixties, migrated to Bedford in the late 1950s when he was only a child. His colleague, Rocco Di Giorgio, aged 60, came to the town only a couple of years later. The Italian-style

---

[7] As already mentioned in Chapter 1, it is important to point out that first generation immigrants from the South of Italy use a Neapolitan-based form of their village dialect which has in turn been transmitted to their children and grandchildren. Standard Italian is not the language normally spoken in the home. Therefore, the Italian language referred to in this study is always a form of the Campania dialect and not Standard Italian.

barber shop is a couple of miles off a main road, in a peaceful residential area. The clientele is very mixed, and they have both BI and British regular customers. More than any of the other workplaces recorded in town, this business represents the archetypal 1950s barber shop in Italy with its traditional décor and atmosphere inside, and tables and chairs outside where elderly men pass the time of day playing cards and chatting.

BED11 "Vincenzo's" is a much more modern ladies' and gents' hairdressing salon. The shop has recently been refurbished and is in a prominent position in the town centre. The owner, Vincenzo Goduti, moved to Bedford in the 1960s at a very early age and settled in the town in the hope of a better future. The salon is family-run and Vincenzo's son helps him out.

BED12 "Giovanni's" is a small unpretentious ladies' and gents' hairdresser's, situated in a quiet area of Bedford, and is less than a mile from the town centre. The owner, Giovanni D'Angelico runs the business with his wife, Rosa. As it is in a quieter area on the outskirts of the town, the shop is less crowded and most of their regular customers are either BI or British.

2.9.2 Problems encountered during data collection

The ethnographic approach has both advantages and disadvantages due to its very nature and a number of problems were encountered during data collection. The first difficulty concerned finding workplaces where recording would be allowed. Despite the proven effectiveness of the "friend of a friend" technique, it is not always foolproof. Through friends, requests for interviews for this academic research were made and some of these requests to some local restaurants were met with hostility or outright refusal on one or two occasions if payment were not offered for their participation. These demands were made because of interviews carried out by local media in the wake of the Italian World Cup victory the scope of which were entirely unrelated to academic research. Nevertheless, this illustrates the difficulties sometimes encountered when using this approach.

CHAPTER THREE

ANALYSIS AND FINDINGS

3.1 Previous findings: the Questionnaire Survey and Informal Interviews

In the course of previous research on the current sociolinguistic situation of Bedford Italians, a questionnaire survey revealed interesting patterns (Guzzo 2005, 2007). The questionnaire was distributed ethnographically, making use of informal network links among friends, acquaintances and church members. A total sample of 63 written questionnaires was distributed randomly to BIs of the second and third generation. More specifically, 37 questionnaires were filled in by adult speakers, 22 questionnaires by teenage informants, and finally, 4 questionnaires by pre-adolescent speakers ≤ 12 years old.

As for gender and cohort, the informants for the questionnaire were as follows (see Table 3-1): 24 male adult speakers of the second generation of Italians in Bedford, 13 second generation female adult speakers, 9 third generation young male speakers, and 17 third generation young female speakers.

The main aim of the survey was to observe the speakers' Italian and English language competence, their ability to indicate how strong their ethnic identity perception was, and to outline their choices of language(s) according to different interlocutors and situations. Based on the answers to the questionnaires (see Appendix for the full questionnaire form), some general conclusions were drawn.

Specifically, an overall set of 14 questions constituted the structure of the questionnaire formulated. The informants were asked to answer each question by choosing the answer they thought to be most appropriate. The first set of 5 questions concerned family structure. Inquiring about the nationality of their grandparents, parents, and partner, its aim was to elicit their family structure and genealogy.

Table 3-1. Distribution of questionnaires among informants.

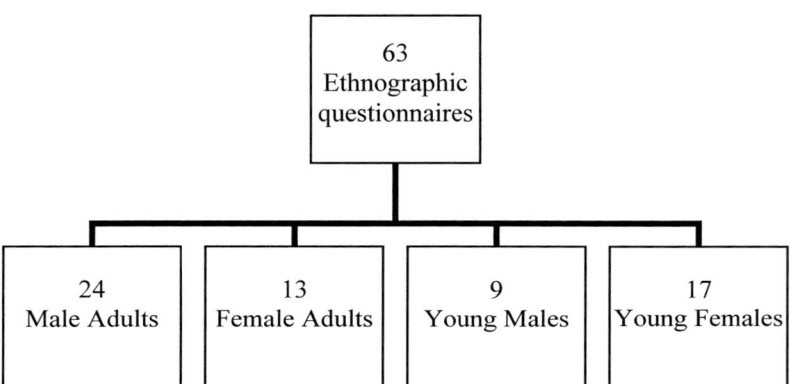

The second set of 4 questions related to the speakers' Italian and English language competence and ability. The aim was to elicit the participants' perception of their level of linguistic competence in Italian and English. They were asked to self-assess their knowledge in both languages by evaluating their speaking, reading, writing, and comprehension skills.

The third set of 2 questions referred to the speakers' exposure to mass media. Informants were asked whether, and how often, they watched Italian or English television, so as to verify the scale of their exposure to the language(s).

The fourth set of 2 questions concerned the speakers' perception of their ethnic identity and heritage. Informants were asked whether and how strongly they felt they were either Italian or English. These questions aimed to determine whether there was a dominant feeling towards one ethnic identity in particular, and to identify the speakers' level of awareness.

The fifth set of questions related to the speakers' choices of language(s) with different interlocutors and in different situations. In the first part of the question, informants were asked which interlocutors they were more likely to use Italian or English with; in the second part, they were asked to relate their language choice to the context, and to say whether in different situations (i.e. at work and at home), they were more likely to use one language or the other (Guzzo 2005, 2007).

3.1.1 Questionnaire findings

As far as the BI informants' self-assessments were concerned, the general consensus was that they have maintained their passive Italian language competence. They claim to socialise with their own community members much more than with British speakers, and as a result, Italian continues to be used (although code-switching is evident on many occasions) and that they have maintained a reasonably good overall linguistic abililty [8].

Some very significant insights come from the questions concerning the speakers' Italian and English language competence which were intended to produce evidence of the level of awareness the speakers have with regard to their speaking, reading, writing and understanding abilities in both languages.

As claimed in previous work (Guzzo 2005, 2007), speakers appeared confident while answering the questions on their English skills. Findings concerning Italian are reported in Table 3-2 below [9].

Second generation male BIs claimed to have a good knowledge of spoken Italian, good Italian reading skills, quite a good level of written Italian, and a good understanding of the language. Second generation female BIs claimed to speak Italian perfectly, to be quite good at reading Italian, quite good at writing, and to understand the language perfectly. As for the young males, their answers show very similar results. The young males stated that they have a good knowledge of spoken Italian (67%), good reading skills, quite a good level of writing, and a good level of understanding Italian. Surprisingly, their female peers claim to be less competent [10]. They report very little speaking ability (41.5%), good reading, quite good writing skills, and perfect (41%) and quite good comprehension (41% of the speakers). The findings show that only the young female speakers have less command of the Italian language.

---

[8] As already mentioned in previous paragraphs, the linguistic competence transmitted by the first generation of immigrants to their children and grandchildren is a Neapolitan-based form of their village dialect. Standard Italian is not the language they are used to speaking at home. Therefore, the Italian referred to is a form of dialect from the Campania region.

[9] Informants were requested to answer four questions concerning their speaking, reading, writing and comprehension skills in Italian. *Not at all (N), very little (V), quite good (QG), good (G), perfectly (P)* were the possible answers.

[10] Questionnaire findings on the young female speakers are fully confirmed by the findings of the analysis of the recordings.

Table 3-2. Percentage distribution of answers to questions 6 to 9 with regard to language competence and skills in Italian.

List of questions	% Adult Male		% Adult Female		% Young Male		% Young Female	
Can you **SPEAK** Italian?	0% :	N	0% :	N	11% :	N	0%:	N
	4% :	V	8% :	V	11% :	V	**41.5% :**	**V**
	35%:	QG	23%:	QG	11%:	QG	17.5%:	QG
	43% :	**G**	23%:	G	**67% :**	**G**	23.5%:	G
	18% :	P	**46%:**	**P**	0% :	P	17.5% :	P
Can you **READ** Italian?	0% :	N	0% :	N	22,5%:	N	0%:	N
	26%:	V	15%:	V	11% :	V	29.5%:	V
	26%:	QG	8%:	QG	0% :	QG	29.5%:	QG
	39%:	**G**	**46%:**	**G**	**55.5%: G**		**35%:**	**G**
	13% :	P	31% :	P	11% :	P	6% :	P
Can you **WRITE** Italian?	9%:	N	0%:	N	22% :	N	6%:	N
	27%:	V	15%:	V	11% :	V	23.5%:	V
	30%: QG		**38.5%: QG**		**44.5%: QG**		**35%: QG**	
	17% :	G	15.5%:	G	22.5% :	G	29.5%:	G
	17% :	P	31% :	P	0% :	P	6% :	P
Can you **UNDER STAND** Italian?	0% :	N	0%:	N	0% :	N	0%:	N
	4% :	V	0%:	V	11% :	V	12%:	V
	17%:	QG	0%:	QG	11%:	QG	**41%: QG**	
	40%:	**G**	38.5%:	G	**55.5%: G**		6%:	G
	39% :	P	**61.%:**	**P**	22.5% :	P	**41% :**	**P**

Concerning the speakers' perception of their ethnic identity and heritage, informants were asked whether and how strongly they felt they were Italian or English. The aim behind these questions was to ascertain if they felt a dominant ethnic identity existed, if present, how strongly it was felt, and their level of awareness of it. As Table 3-3 shows[11], in response to the question "Do you feel Italian? How strongly?" both male and female speakers, adult and young alike, answered "yes, extremely". The data relating to young female speakers were not very different from the male results, but their feeling of "Italianness" seems to be less strong. Again, young female Bedford Italians show that they are more removed from the language than the other groups of speakers.

---

[11] Informants were requested to answer two questions concerning their ethnic identity perception. *Extremely (E), very (V), Quite (Q), very little (VL), not at all (N)* were the possible answers.

Table 3-3. Percentage distribution of answers to questions 12 and 13 with regard to the speakers' ethnic identity perception.

List of questions	% Adult Male	% Adult Female	% Young Male	% Young Female
Do you feel **ITALIAN?** If so, how strongly?	**43%:** E 35%: V 22%: Q 0%: VL 0%: N	**46.5%:** E 23%: V 30.5%: Q 0%: VL 0%: N	**55.5%:** E 22.5%: V 0%: Q 22%: VL 0%: N	23.5%: E **65%:** V 11.5%: Q 0%: VL 0% : N
Do you feel **ENGLISH?** If so, how strongly?	9% : E 9% : V **30%:** Q 26%: VL 26%: N	0%: E 30.5%: V 30.5%: Q 0%: VL **39%:** N	0% : E 11%: V 22.5%: Q 22%: VL **44.5%:** N	6%: E 12%: V **29.5%:** Q **29.5%:** VL 23% : N

As far as English identity is concerned, the results show that the overall reported feeling of "Englishness" is weak, with both 2nd and 3rd generation informants showing similar findings. It is important to note that Bedford Italians who speak English as L1 have spent their entire lives in England. Despite the fact that their language competence is much stronger in English than in Italian, since their environment is English-speaking and the Bedford Italians are perfectly well integrated, these speakers generally perceive themselves as Italian. In most cases, they feel they are English only to a very slight degree. Second generation male informants state they feel quite English (30%), while 39% of their female counterparts, on the contrary, say they do not feel English; third-generation male speakers are even further along the scale with 44.5% saying they do not feel at all English, and, although their female peers are always slightly closer to the English world and more integrated, they admit to feeling quite/very little English (cf. Table 3-3 above).

Besides revealing that Italian and English-speaking Bedfordians claimed to have quite a good knowledge of Italian. The questionnaire findings showed perhaps more interestingly, that as far as the speakers' level of ethnic identity perception is concerned, the informants perceived themselves to be Italian and not English. Their cultural heritage is strongly felt and well consolidated. Significantly, although the informants were born and brought up in England by first or second generation Italian parents, they think of themselves as Italians in Britain or at least they were concerned to report themselves as such to me (an investigator from the home country).

As for the last set of questions, the focus was on the speakers' choice of language(s) according to different interlocutors and contexts. In the first part of the question set, informants were asked with which interlocutor they were more likely to use Italian or English; in the second part, they were asked to relate their language choice to the context, and answer whether, in different situations, at work, at school or at home, they were more likely to use one language or the other. The following tables contain answers with reference to the workplace, which appear more relevant for the current investigation.

Table 3-4. Percentage distribution of answers to question 14 with regard to the speakers' choices of Italian according to different interlocutors in the workplace or at school.

List of questions	% Adult Male	% Adult Female	% Young Male	% Young Female
What language (s) do/did you use in each situation?	49%: Colleagues 37%: Customers 29%: The Boss	23%: Colleagues 23%: Customers 15%: The Boss	33%: Teachers 55%: Classmates 22%: Taking Notes	35.5%: Teachers 24%: Classmates 12%: Taking Notes

Table 3-5. Percentage distribution of answers to question 14 with regard to the speakers' choices of English according to different interlocutors in the workplace or at school.

List of questions	% Adult Male	% Adult Female	% Young Male	% Young Female
What language (s) do/did you use in each situation?	87.5%: Colleagues 82%: Customers 54%: The Boss	85%: Colleagues 77%: Customers 69%: The Boss	100%: Teachers 89%: Classmates 66%: Taking Notes	88.5%: Teachers 65%: Classmates 82.5%: Taking Notes

Comparing Table 3-4 and 3-5 with regard to the use of Italian versus English in the workplace or at school, Italian is used in the workplace quite significantly, especially with colleagues, and with customers. While

Diglossic use of Eng and Ite

at work, the adult male informants use Italian with their colleagues (49%) more than their female counterparts (23%). Presumably, depending on the job activity, their colleagues are very likely to be BIs too. On the other hand, adult female speakers behave similarly but with a less frequent use, as the above percentages show.

As far as the young male informants are concerned, they are more likely to use Italian while speaking to their classmates (55%) than while taking notes (22%), although they might also use Italian with their teachers (33%). Their female peers, on the other hand, are more likely to use Italian with teachers (35.5%) than classmates (24%). Surprisingly the results are quite different but may have been due to interpretation of the question itself. A reasonable assumption might be that the girls answered the question thinking it referred to their Italian language class. This is plausible and would explain the different results.

On the other hand, as for the use of English according to the same contexts and interlocutors, as in Table 3-5, English is undoubtedly the language most often adopted and the first choice for the informants. There are no doubts that at work, as well as at school, both adult and young BI speakers choose English in these situations with these interlocutors.

In conclusion, Italian is still in use, above all at home and with members of the same ethnic group, although English proved to be more spoken mainly at work, at school, in formal administrative settings and among acquaintances. The speakers tend to keep the two languages separate, using one at a time, as in a diglossic situation. Although not discussed explicitly here, the questionnaire survey, as well as the recordings, also reveal that the informants code-switch, especially if their interlocutor does so (Guzzo 2005).

3.1.2 Informal Interviews

In linguistics, the transfer of linguistic items from one language to another through contact is very significant, as it enriches the structure of both donor and recipient languages. In the final sample of informants a number of variables were examined. These included the social variables of age, gender and duration of residence in Britain, and the linguistic variables of the FACE vowel and the de-aspiration of the plosives /p, t, k/. The sample who participated in the second part of the 2004 investigation consisted of 12 male and female teenagers including Italian-English and British-English speakers. This stage of the study was aimed primarily at revealing whether *Italian* influenced the *English* of the third generation community members and whether some evidence of this influence existed in the speech of the informants (Guzzo 2005, 2007).

Generally speaking, as Bedford is part of the South East of England, either the diphthong [ɛi] or [æi] of the FACE vowel were expected to be found in the speech of these informants. On the contrary, analysis revealed a tendency towards the realisation of a mid-close front position [eɪ]. As for the consonant variable, recent work in sociolinguistics has shown that what at first sight seems to be free variation in the plosives, may actually be a consequence of other factors (Wells 1982). The variation in the *aspiration* of the voiceless plosive may be determined by stylistic factors or social circumstances. Finally, both the selected variables can be considered evidence of linguistic variation in BIC English. Arguably, this variation may be the reflection of their Italian heritage in the language of the informants.

The frequency and distribution of the two variables examined varied strikingly from one speaker to another. However, it is legitimate to suggest that the young males may be identified by some features while the girls are characterised by a different trend. As Figure 3-1 illustrates, the boys' data show a strong preference for [eɪ] in any environment where the diphthong variation is possible. The frequency of the variation from the standard form [ɛɪ], or the South Eastern variant [æi], in favour of [eɪ] is higher than 50% in all the four male informant recordings, whereas the female speakers never exceed 50%. Although the variation is widespread in both male and female speech, the latter are more likely to retain the standard form [ɛɪ]. This might suggest that BIC female speakers are more integrated into local British society than the male informants.

As Figure 3-2 shows, the de-aspiration of the voiceless plosives /p, t, k/ in preceding stressed vowel environments is certainly quite widespread in both the male and female speech recorded, the level of variation never exceeding 30%; nonetheless, this feature can be considered a marked characteristic of a variety that might be referred to as *Italian-accented*. BIC informants showed a preference for using de-aspirated forms of plosives in both linguistic environments of preceding stressed and unstressed vowels, thus placing themselves in the *non-standard* camp of speakers of ethnic minorities. Interestingly, de-aspiration might also be an indicator used to signal membership of a minority group. In this respect, a pan-ethnic dialect may be emerging that shares similar features despite being used among different ethnic groups, and BIC speech may well represent an example of this phenomenon (Guzzo 2005, 2007).

Figure 3-1. The FACE Variable ɛɪ ~ eɪ with regard to gender.

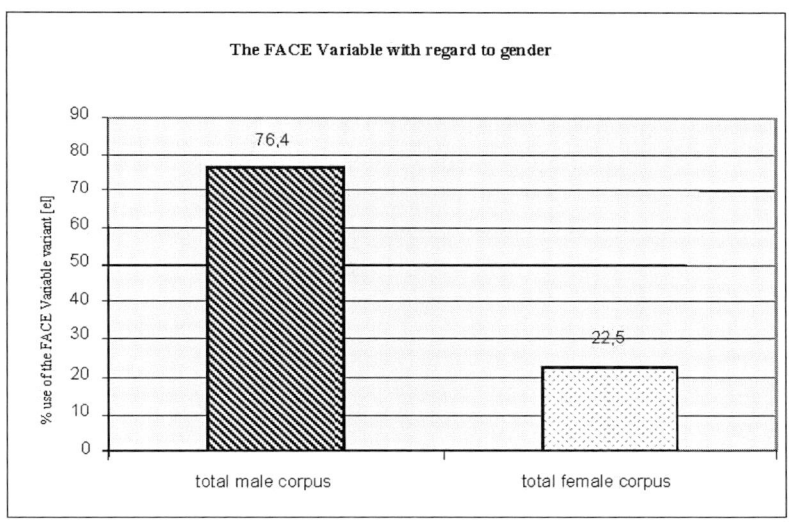

Figure 3-2. The de-aspiration of plosives with regard to gender.

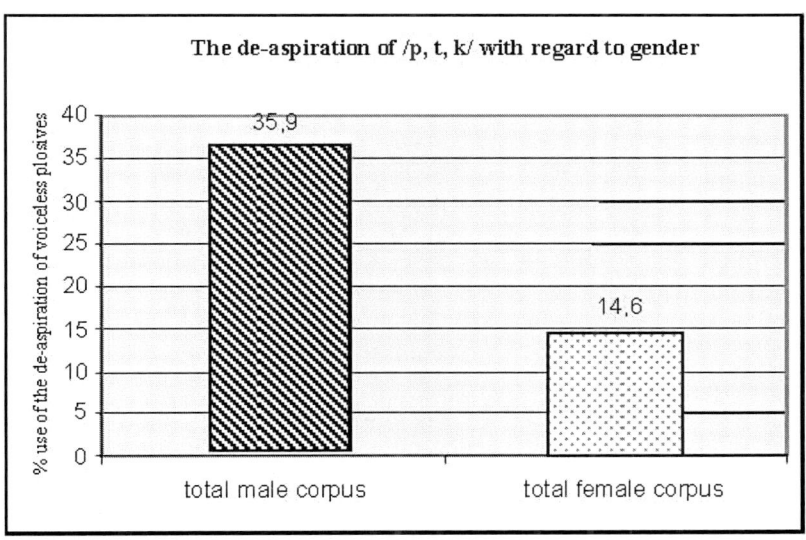

According to the data analysed, it was possible to conclude that the study revealed the informants' tendency towards the mid-close front position [eɪ]; the speakers' glide begins from slightly above the mid-open front position [ɛɪ], and moves towards the mid-close front [eɪ]. As for the variation in the *aspiration* of the voiceless plosives, this turned out to be determined by stylistic factors and/or social circumstances. The *de-aspiration* of the plosives present in the speech of the informants seems to indicate that the process of de-aspiration is the result of Italian influence on the English language. Arguably, this variation might also represent a feature of a pan-ethnic dialect emerging in British English within minority groups in Great Britain (Britain 2005, Britain and Fox 2006, Fox 2006, Guzzo, Fox and Britain forthcoming) since it has also been shown to be present in other research projects on Pakistani and Bangladeshi.

The teenage males turned out to be more willing to adopt non-standard features of *English* than their female counterparts. Young male Bedford Italians tend to use more *non-standard* vowels and *Italian*-influenced features in their speech, while their female peers articulate the vowels and aspirate the plosive consonants in a more *southern British English* related manner. Thus, on the basis of the findings reported here, the male informants seem to be further along the way towards a variation which could represent the first step towards the formation of *Bedford Italian English* (Guzzo 2005, 2007).

3.2 The 2006 study: Linguistic Variables

For the 2006 study, two phonological and three morphological variables were investigated. Following Charles Boberg's approach (1997), the phonological variable, *foreign (a)* (as in *pasta, lasagne,* and *latte,* for instance) was selected together with a frequently occurring cluster of phonemes isolated in Italian loanwords when code-switched into English. As for the three morphological variables submitted for linguistic analysis, (1) the formation of plurals in Anglicised Italian lexis, (2) the presence/absence of inversion in question formation, and (3) the presence/absence of third person singular present-tense marking were chosen.

3.2.1 Foreign (a) and Charles Boberg's approach

The examination of the pronunciation of /a/ in foreign loanwords in English was pioneered by Charles Boberg (1997) in the US. Foreign (a) nativization is extremely variable and involves thousands of lexical items.

I would have expected it to have been researched, described and explained in previous studies, but there has been little research and only a limited amount of references before Boberg's work. Using Wells' lexical set (Labov, 1973; Wells, 1982), foreign (a) refers to the PALM-CLASS-TRAP type. As he comments:

> "[…] the membership of this [palm-class] lexical set is unusual and difficult to circumscribe. No more than a handful of really common everyday words belong to it unambiguously, e.g. *father*. Most of the *palm* words are recent borrowings from foreign languages in which the foreign [a]-type vowel is rendered as the *palm* vowel, e.g. *sonata, rajah*. But uncertainty arises through the fact that the trap vowel is also used to render foreign-language [a]. Thus for example *pasta* and *Nicaragua* usually have stressed /æ/ in Britain, but /ɑː/ in the United States, while conversely *morale* and *Iran* usually have /ɑː/ in Britain and /æ/ in the United States".
> (1982: 142)

Wells' lexical set (Labov, 1973; Wells, 1982), makes a reference to the phenomenon of foreign (a), but his comments are limited by the small corpus of words he considers. Boberg (1997) on the basis of experimental and word-list data, leads the way by investigating the phonological nativization of foreign words spelt with <a>, such as *pasta, tobacco, mango*, for instance, to verify how the foreign vowel [a] was produced in both British and American English. The possible realisations are two English phonemes: short /æ/ (as in *cat*) and long /ɑː/ (as in *father*). His aim is not only to describe the variation but also to create a model of nativization of foreign (a) for each of the above-mentioned varieties of English. In order to analyse the trend diachronically, Boberg selects a random sample of foreign (a) words from a British and an American standard dictionary, the Oxford English Dictionary and the Merriam-Webster Dictionary respectively, from which he selects a database of 847 tokens for his diachronic analysis. The study shows that foreign (a) nativization patterns were established in the 18th century, reporting three main outcomes: /æ/ as in *cat*, /ɑː/ (as in *father*) and a variant form-between these vowels. More specifically, analysing 360 tokens borrowed after the 18th century the findings reveal important differences in the frequency of each result with respect to British and American English: British nativization displays 70% /æ/, 26% /ɑː/ and 4% variation, whereas American nativization shows 51% /æ/, 31% /ɑː/ and 18% variation.

In addition, other methods of investigations were used by Boberg to show that the lexical distribution of the results is not accidental. A range of surveys were carried out and results produced a probabilistic model of lexical variation for which British and American nativization were shown to differ according to systematic outcomes. In British nativization, due to prosodic factors, /æ/ is the default vowel, appearing repeatedly in closed syllables, whereas /ɑː/ is regular in open syllables. On the other hand, surprisingly, American nativization, although starting with /æ/ as the default vowel, shows a trend toward /ɑː/ in both open and closed syllables. Boberg concludes that the reasons for this variation are due to–the qualitative nature of American nativization versus the quantitative nature of British English; /æ/ and /ɑː/ in the pronunciation of /a/ in foreign loanwords into English differ according to their phonological properties of quantity and quality.

3.2.2 Foreign (a) and Anglicised Italian lexis

Adopting Boberg's nativization model as the basis for my investigation with respect to the pronunciation of foreign (a) in Italian lexis, some questions arose.

For an immigrant community of speakers such as Bedford Italians, what could emerge from an analysis of their pronunciation of foreign (a) within the speech of three generations of speakers in an audience design framework? What happens to foreign (a) when English is produced by people of non-English ethnicity in a specific English setting such as that of service encounters?

In order to investigate the trend of this quite obscure phonological variable within my present corpus, I modified the model proposed by Boberg, contrasting three possible realisations of the (a) variable: the two British English phonemes, short /ɑː/ (as in *cat*) and long back /ɑː/ (as in *father*) versus the Italian phoneme, short front /a/ (as in the Italian pronunciation of *pasta*). A total number of 555 tokens in its Italian and British pronunciations were detected and analysed according to the interlocutor and audience type. Considering Boberg's results for foreign (a) nativization in British English, either phoneme /æ/ or /ɑː/ was expected from Bedfordian speakers, although speakers retaining original Italian pronunciation were expected to articulate a shorter and fronter rather than the back long vowel /ɑː/.

In light of the analysis of foreign (a), another phonological variable was also selected for the investigation. If Italian (a) shows interesting articulations according to the interlocutors and the audience setting, what happens more generally to Italian lexis? Will words of Italian origin, such as *latte* or *cappuccino*, be Anglicised? Will possible Anglicisation of Italian lexis vary according to style, interlocutors and context? In order to verify the pronunciation of a cluster of Italian words, 898 tokens were detected and examined. Each pronunciation is encoded as IT (Italian), EN (English) or MIX (when a mixed pronunciation was displayed).

As mentioned above, the transfer of linguistic items from one language to another through contact enriches both donor and recipient languages and has been widely discussed in historical and contemporary linguistics (Weinreich, 1968; Hock, 1986; Thomason and Kaufman, 1988; Koch, 2002). Traditionally, borrowings are most commonly lexical borrowings, where the source language transfers lexical items, also defined as loanwords, to the recipient language. As in Boberg (1997), through a process of phonetic and phonological adaptation, borrowings are usually followed by a process of nativization. Therefore, when a loanword is nativized, the donor language phonemes that it contains will match the recipient language phonemes either by showing phonetic similarity, matching spelling or matching morphologically. As far as the pronunciation of loanwords is concerned, when the foreign phoneme is reproduced in the recipient language, it does not necessarily match with a native phoneme, unless both languages share the same phoneme. Only in a few cases, does repeated imitation lead to integration (van Coetsem as in Boberg 1997), and on those occasions, the foreign phone enters into the recipient language as a new phoneme.

One of the aims of the present research is to examine instances of both foreign (a) and a cluster of other mixed phonemes from the source language, i.e. Italian, in the English of a well-established Italian community of speakers in the UK in order to verify whether a process of Anglicization applies to all Italian borrowings used by three generations of BIs in specific contexts of use and when interacting with either Italian or British speakers.

3.3 Morphological variables

There have been a more limited number of studies concerning morphological variation in British English than those concerning phonological investigations, and fewer still have contributed quantitatively to the analysis of grammatical features. Recently, thanks to access to larger corpora, more systematic analyses have been carried out, at least for some non-standard features of the language (Britain, 2007). One of the main difficulties when attempting to study morphological variation lies in the necessity of having a corpus large enough to contain a sufficient number of instances to analyse. Some morphological features only occur very rarely in speech and analyses need appropriate corpora so as to be able to find out more about their linguistic distribution.

Previous studies have mainly regarded L1 influence on SLA, and have been more experimental, often concentrating on the "classroom language testing" approaches of SLA. Most studies have focussed on the errors[12] that reflect the influence of a speaker's native language on second language acquisition. Particularly, Hagège (1999) claims that the power of L1 can be observed in children's as well as in adults' L2. Interference between L1 and L2 in children will not become permanent as long as children have sufficient exposure to L2, whereas in adult speakers L1 influence will appear to increase constantly as a monolingual adult gets older, since his or her L1 structures will impose themselves on any other language which that person may want to learn. It is worth noting that in the process of acquiring a second language, L2 learners will unconsciously make up structures influenced by some L1 knowledge they already possess and this can lead to errors.

Besides studies of L1 transfer in general, there have been numerous SLA specific investigations concerning English learning, but none working on naturalistic L2 data. To name a few, Thanh Ha Nguyen (1995) investigated Vietnamese learners, a case study in which he examined English past tense marking, noting the existence and discussing the role of L1 transfer in the acquisition of English; and Lakkis and Malak (2000) researched the transfer of Arabic prepositions into English by Arab students. Register and pronunciation have also been investigated in SLA with regard to some L1 influence or transfer. Hagège (1996) discusses the influence of L1 on accent and, suggesting that there is a critical age for language acquisition, especially for the acquisition of a native-like accent, he notes that the ear acts like a filter, and after the critical age of 11, he claims, it only accepts sounds that belong to one's own native language.

Using the 65.000-word corpus available to me, it was decided that three morphological features would be the basis of this research and through the adoption of sociolinguistic methods of analysis the following were found to be of particular importance and examined: (1) the formation of plurals in Anglicised Italian lexis, (2) the presence/absence of inversion in question formation, and (3) the presence/absence of third person singular present tense verb marking.

---

[12] Corder (1967) was the first to introduce the distinction between *errors* (in competence) and *mistakes* (in performance). This definition of *errors* shall be adopted throughout the present research.

3.3.1 Plurality marking on Italian nouns

Plurality marking on nouns in variationist literature is not a well researched feature and needs further analysis. Studies have shown that many varieties of English have neglected to mark plurality on nouns (Cheshire et al 1989, Hughes & Trudgill 1979, Trudgill 2003, Watts 2006, Beal 2004 as in Britain 2007). For instance, as Britain notes in the following examples, plurality is not always marked:

> *(1) "That's three mile away from here*
> *(2) I need four foot of polythene sheet*
> *(3) Two pound of plums, please!"* (Britain 2007:110)

In the case of the present research, interesting patterns have emerged. As a consequence of the phonological analysis carried out on the Anglicisation of Italian lexis, plurality has only been considered in regard to the list of tokens selected for the phonological investigation. The aim is to show whether, and how, English plurality is marked on loanwords from Italian in the speech of the three generations of BIs. Traditionally, nouns are inflected for grammatical number i.e., singular or plural. The rule concerning the plural formation of borrowings says that a suffix -s is added to the singular form.

What happens then in the speech of BIs as far as plurality marking on nouns is concerned? Is there any variation according to style, interlocutor and setting? Assuming the standard rule for plurality, the plural formation of Italian loanwords has been analysed and discussed.

3.3.2 Presence/absence of inversion in question formation

AUX- and WH-question formation have been studied extensively in English. Concerning wh-questions, Ross (1967) formulated island constraints on transformations and Chomsky (1977) showed, on the basis of a variety of constructions, how it is possible to identify the application of wh-movement by means of a set of diagnostic properties. As conventionally known, there are two basic types of questions in English: "Yes/No" questions, which ask for a positive or negative answer, and wh-questions, which ask for specific information and start with a question word. The most basic (and earliest) rule was simple: invert the order of the subject and any tensed verb or auxiliary.

The most common wh-question structure is: Question word + Auxiliary Verb + Object or Main Verb. The formation used with wh-questions depends on whether the topic under discussion is the subject or predicate of a sentence. For the subject pattern, we simply replace the person/object being asked about with the appropriate wh-word (e.g. Something is bothering you. What is bothering you?). To make a question using the predicate pattern, we form a question by inverting the subject and (first) auxiliary verb. Then, add the appropriate wh- word to the beginning of the sentence (e.g. They have been somewhere. Where have they been?).

This study investigates different instances of the presence/absence of inversion in question formation. Questions using the wh-words (what, who, when, where, why, and how), in singular and plural verb forms in the English of BIs with respect to inter-speaker variation and audience type throw light on interesting patterns of the BIs' speech. In rating the results, inversion (e.g. Do you want a coffee?) and non-inversion (e.g. You got any mustard?) of AUX-question formation are reported as standard, whereas rates of non-inversion in wh-clauses (e.g. What they'll do?) are reported as non-standard. Possible reasons for this discrepancy are discussed.

3.3.3 Presence/absence of third person singular present tense marking

The use of 3rd person -s, while well researched in the more experimental and "classroom language testing" approaches of SLA, is again not one that has been thoroughly examined in naturalistic L2 data of this kind.

The production of third-person -s in English verbs seems to be very debated. Many studies have contrasted varieties of English showing different trends. For instance, compared to Mainstream American English (MAE), in African American English (AAE), -s is rarely supplied. Experimental studies in both LA and SLA have often reported on third-person -s, as for instance, De Villiers & Johnson (2007) explored what information children get solely from -s at the end of a verb. Thanks to a sample of sixty-five MAE- and sixty-five AAE-speaking four to seven-year-old children, they show that neither group of four-year-olds could use the -s to determine if the event was generic rather than past tense on a verb (e.g. *cuts/cut*), or whether it was a verb or a noun compound as in *The penguin dresses/The penguin dress*. MAE-speakers are shown not to use the information in third person -s alone until age five, and not reliably until the age of six, whereas AAE-speaking children proved not to use the information in -s at all in this age range.

Moreover, trying to give an explanation for the phenomenon, some scholars treat the issue as an instance of loss and/or reinterpretation of markers, others as a case of failure of the third person markers to develop. According to Haiman (1985) and Croft (1990), as in Siewierska (2005), the main reason for the zero marking of third person verbal forms lies in the principle of economy, for which there is a tendency for speakers to shorten linguistic expressions. Other explanations claim (Koch 1995 as in Siewierska 2005), that "there is a strong tendency in languages to reinterpret third person verbal forms as part of the stem or as tense markers". This tendency follows Benveniste's view (1971 as in Siewierska 2005), for which the third person is "cognitively a non-person", a reason for which it should also be unmarked morphologically. Lastly, Ariel (2000 as in Siewierska 2005) argues that third person forms simply did not develop.

In the present investigation, given that person markers typically combine person distinctions with those of number, a list of BI tokens of present tense verbal -s exhibits number distinction with regard to the third person, for which zero might suggest a nativised second language form, as in Trudgill's study of East Anglian English (1998).

3.4 Analysis

It has already been established that the main aim of the present work is to investigate phonological and morphological variables in the language of three generations of BIs in the workplace. In order to do so, 20 hours of naturally occurring workplace language were ethnographically collected and all speakers whose ethnicity was not certain were discarded, in order to maintain strict comparability within the corpus. The final sample consists of 100 participants of Italian ethnicity, belonging to the three generations of BIs, either customers or workers in the fields of catering services, sales and hairdressing as shown in Table 3-6 below.

Table 3-6. Business size.

No. of people per business	Business
8	BED01
9	BED02
7	BED03+BED04
13	BED05
5	BED06
6	BED07
15	BED08
2	BED09
23	BED10
9	BED11
3	BED12
TOTAL **100**	

The evaluation of the 4 linguistic variables will be descriptive, highlighting the extent to which BI speakers may be termed to have shown variation. A complete analysis of all tokens for each of the variables analysed.

The four linguistic variables:

Phonological Variables	–	Foreign (a) => [æ] [ɑː] or [a];
	–	**Anglicised Italian Lexis**
Morphological Variables	**1.** Lexis;	**Plural marking in Anglicised Italian**
	2.	**Question Formation;**
	3.	**Third Person –s**

As far as the social index is concerned, detailed references regarding the informants' social status and gender were disregarded and considered irrelevant for the present research. However, what was taken into consideration was the variable of age, as far as the three generations of BIs are concerned, and also ethnicity. Table 3-7 below shows the representation of the three generations in each of the recordings;

Table 3-7. Generation cohorts.

No. of people per generation			Business
1st	2nd	3rd	
-	8	-	BED01
-	6	3	BED02
2	3	2	BED03+BED04
1	9	3	BED05
-	3	2	BED06
-	3	3	BED07
-	14	1	BED08
2	-	-	BED09
1	7	15	BED10
1	6	2	BED11
2	-	1	BED12
TOTAL	**9**	**59**	**32**	

Table 3-8, the overall number of informants, grouped according to generation, in each of the three job categories identified for the analysis.

Table 3-8. Employment sub-categories.

No. of people per business	Restaurants	Sellers	Hairdressers
No. of people per generation:			
1st generation	2	2	5
2nd generation	33	20	6
3rd generation	23	6	3
TOTAL	**58**	**28**	**14**

In addition, each recording is analysed according to intra- and inter-speaker variation and audience type, aiming at verifying whether variation occurred in the case of Italian versus British interlocutors, and contrasting the different workplace settings. After comparing the speech of participants according to the variables selected, their characteristics will be examined, interpreted and discussed. A set of twenty-one tables and sixteen graphs will display how BI speakers communicate and interact with regard to audience design. Generations and interlocutor ethnicity are ranked on the horizontal axis, while a list of variants are placed on the vertical axis in the figures.

3.4.1 Informants

As pointed out in the previous chapter and illustrated in Tables 3-6, 3-7 and 3-8 above, the final sample of the 11 businesses which were recorded for the investigation are grouped according to their job categories. The label *Restaurants* is given to the Bedford Italian businesses specifically including: BED01 the kiosk "La Piazza", BED02 (grouped as a single entity because both recordings referred to the same restaurant) "Cappuccino Bar"; BED05 the take-away pizzeria "Chirico's"; BED06 the restaurant "La Dolce Vita"; and BED10 the restaurant pizzeria "Santaniello's". The label *Sellers* refers to the workplace settings of wholesalers, retailers, and market traders: BED03-BED04 the market stall "Chirico's"; BED07 the wholesaler "AB Fruit"; and BED08 the wholesale bakery "La Rondine", which deals with catering services, such as banqueting for ceremonies. Finally, as for the third and last category of workplace datasets labelled *Hairdressers,* this refers to barber shops and hairdressers: BED09 the barber shop "Tony's"; BED11 the ladies' and gents' hairstylist "Vincenzo's"; and BED12 the hairdresser/barber shop "Giovanni's".

My analysis starts with an illustration of the results according to each linguistic variable within the workplace framework. Each table is followed by a description of the variation of that particular generation in that specific context, and whether informants are interacting with British or Italian interlocutors. A summary of the overall patterns of the informants will be given and discussed after each workplace has been examined separately.

3.5 Findings and Results

3.5.1 Finding Ia: Anglicised Italian Lexis

Findings regarding the phonology of the BIs are divided into two stages according to the two phonological variables analysed: *finding Ia* and *finding Ib*. First of all, the results are analysed and discussed as far as the Anglicised or non-Anglicised Italian lexis is concerned; second, one specific phonological feature of the speech of the three generations of BIs, is elicited i.e. the articulation of foreign /a/. Quantification of this and the other features in this study is by way of an index of the number of tokens according to each of the three generations of speakers, as displayed in the table. The index counts the occurrences of the variable, in this case words of Italian origin, which are Anglicised or non-Anglicised or showing a mixed pronunciation according to an Italian versus British interlocutor. The number of tokens displayed for each of the variants are then multiplied by 100 and divided by the total number of occurrences produced by the speakers of each generation. This gives the exact percentage of actual pronunciation or use for each of the variants displayed by speakers and this is shown in a figure that follows.

The frequency and distribution of the variables examined vary dramatically from one generation of speakers to another, showing a different use of the variables with different interlocutors more frequently rather than in different working contexts. However, it is legitimate to suggest that each generation, as well as each workplace, may be characterised by interesting trends. As far as the Anglicisation of Italian words is concerned, as Table 3-9 and Figure 3-3 illustrate, findings report the number of occurrences in the *restaurant* workplace.

Table 3-9. Anglicised Italian lexis index of tokens in the *Restaurant* workplace.

INTERLOCUTOR	ITALIAN			BRITISH		
GENERATION	1st	2nd	3rd	1st	2nd	3rd
ITALIAN PRONUNCIATION	42	140	48	1	6	3
MIXED PRONUNCIATION	4	7	8	1	2	3
ENGLISH PRONUNCIATION	24	57	67	-	25	4
TOTAL	70	204	123	2	33	10

If the interlocutor is Italian, 1st generation BIs use more Italianized pronunciation of Italian words, whereas if the interlocutor is British, albeit far less frequently[13], it is legitimate to say they tend to maintain

---

[13] Sometimes there is an insufficient number of occurrences to allow conclusions to be drawn. Adopting an ethnographic method has its pros and cons because this aims at obtaining the most natural language and does not seek to control the development of the linguistic exchanges in favour of spontaneity, which means that there is a greater risk of low numbers of specific occurrences in natural and spontaneous interactions. Nonetheless, results show the actual trend.

an Italian articulation of words. Quite predictably the 1st generation is more likely to maintain an Italian accent, yet a considerable amount of English pronunciation (34.3%) is found in the articulation of Italian loanwords, such as *pasta* and *pizza* for instance, despite the presence of an

Figure 3-3. Anglicised Italian lexis results displayed by percentage in the *Restaurant* workplace.

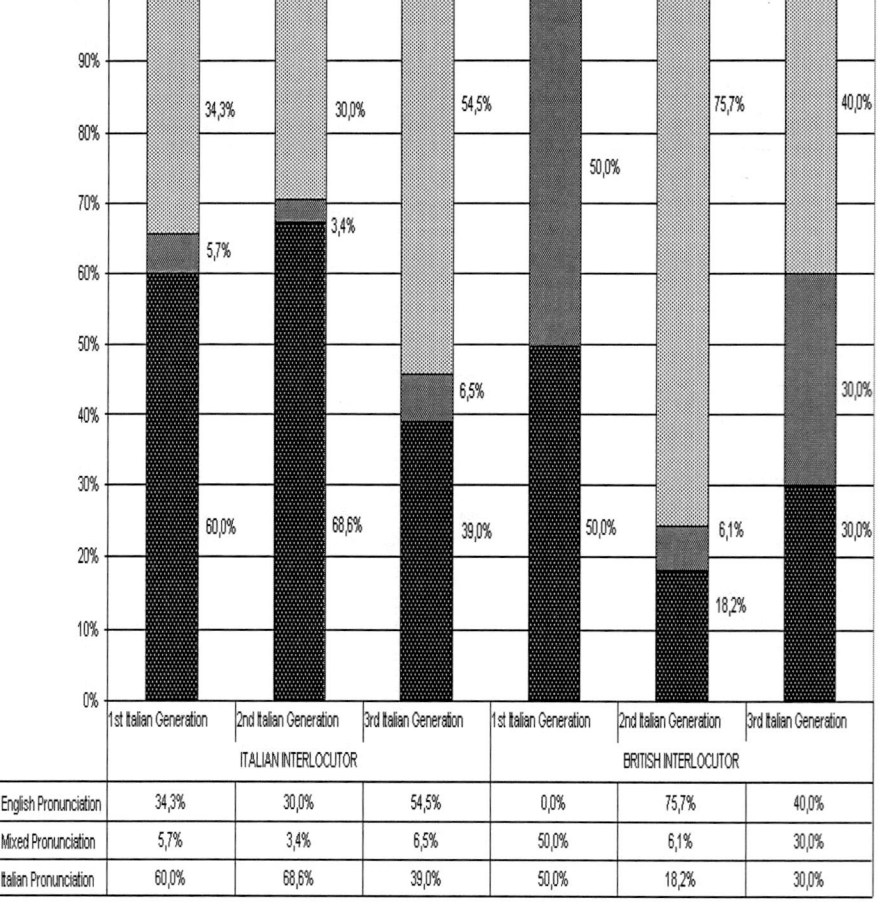

Anglicised Italian Lexis (Restaurants)

	1st Italian Generation	2nd Italian Generation	3rd Italian Generation	1st Italian Generation	2nd Italian Generation	3rd Italian Generation
	ITALIAN INTERLOCUTOR			BRITISH INTERLOCUTOR		
English Pronunciation	34,3%	30,0%	54,5%	0,0%	75,7%	40,0%
Mixed Pronunciation	5,7%	3,4%	6,5%	50,0%	6,1%	30,0%
Italian Pronunciation	60,0%	68,6%	39,0%	50,0%	18,2%	30,0%

Italian interlocutor. It is worth bearing this result in mind when comparing the workplaces, since data from *sellers* and *hairdressers* do not seem to follow the same pattern, as we will see in the following paragraphs.

What is more, 2nd generation BIs in the *Restaurant* workplace show the highest recurrencies of both Italian pronunciation (68.6%) to Italian interlocutors, and English (75.7%) to Anglo-Bedfordians. It seems that compared to the other generations of speakers, 2nd generation BIs are keener on Anglicisation of Italian loanwords when the interlocutor is British, as well as clearly tending towards Italianisation when the interlocutor is Italian. Informants in this case use what they consider – consciously or unconsciously – the most appropriate accent for their audience, therefore shifting markedly from an Italian accent to a British accent according to the ethnicity of customers or colleagues. By doing so, they are accommodating the type of accent they assume to be more suitable, and they are also demonstrating their level of bilingualism.

On the other hand, the 3rd generation speakers show different patterns. Their level of Anglicisation of Italian lexis used with Italians is surprisingly high (54.5%) versus the least marked level of Italianisation (39%). Anglicisation displayed to British customers or colleagues is quite consistent (40%), and 3rd generation informants appear to be the least affected by audience design. Their results in the *Restaurant* workplace show a completely different style. As shown in previous work (Guzzo 2007; Guzzo, Fox and Britain, forthcoming), 3rd generation BIs seem to be affected by different trends and behave unlike 1st and 2nd generation Italians. The patterns shown in the analysis of Anglicisation of Italian words conform to an interpretation of the feature as a marker of Italian identity particularly for the 2nd generation when interacting with Italians, also showing the highest levels of style-shift as predicted by audience.

It can now be assessed how these findings bear on other audience types, by discussing the results of another workplace where the BIs were recorded, i.e. the *Seller*.

As Table 3-10 and Figure 3-4 present, the results appear significantly different compared to those analysed with regard to *Restaurants*. First, the data in this setting show a low token number with regard to 1st and 3rd generations when interacting with British interlocutors. As previously mentioned, low token numbers, as well as the absence of representatives from one or two of the generations, can arise when collecting naturally occurring data. Aiming at the spontaneousness of the language under investigation and making use of ethnographic recordings, not standardised interviews, the setting cannot be arranged nor managed on the basis of any preordained scheme. Therefore, what happened was that on some occasions,

Table 3-10. Anglicised Italian lexis index of tokens in the *Seller* workplace

INTERLOCUTOR	ITALIAN			BRITISH		
GENERATION	1st	2nd	3rd	1st	2nd	3rd
ITALIAN PRONUNCIATION	5	132	15	-	9	-
MIXED PRONUNCIATION	-	12	2	-	4	-
ENGLISH PRONUNCIATION	-	66	9	-	16	-
TOTAL	5	210	26	-	29	-

certain words or expressions were not used by some speakers belonging to one generation or the other, and on other occasions, BIs of one specific generation were not present at the recording[14]. The results demonstrate that 1st generation speakers Italianize all Italian words (100%) when the interlocutor is Italian, whereas 3rd generation informants appear more homogeneous, showing a significant use of Italian pronunciation (56.7%), but also an interesting use of Anglicisation (31.4%) when interacting with Italians. As for 2nd generation informants, the patterns show, that as expected, they Italianize (62.9%) when speaking with Italians and Anglicise (55.2%) when interacting with the British. What is really interesting is that these patterns do not conform with those found in 2nd generation BIs in the *Restaurant* setting. Unlike staff in the pizzerias, kiosks or restaurants, 2nd generation BI salesmen and women show lower levels of frequency according to the interlocutor's ethnicity. Whether interacting with British co-workers or customers, 2nd generation informants of the *Seller* service display a remarkable level of non-Anglicisation (31%), whereas the same generation of participants in the group, are likely to Italianise at much lower levels (18.2%). It can be hypothesized that a possible reason could lie in the specific purposes of the business activity, for which workers in *Restaurants* shift from an Italian to a British pronunciation depending on the interlocutors. They shift as a strategic device when dealing with customers, in a conscious or

---

[14] The methodology with regard to the setting, as in Chapter III, involved collecting workplace language while trying not to interfere with normal work activities in the business where recording was taking place. The methodology was designed to give participants maximum control over the data collection process. Therefore, after positioning the device and starting recording, informants were left to get on with their work, sometimes under observation from a short distance. At times I left the area, while on other occasions I was directly involved in conversations, depending on the informants' requests and comfort levels.

unconscious attempt to get closer to the interlocutor and achieve their business objective which is to make as many sales as possible.

Figure 3-4. Anglicised Italian lexis results displayed by percentage in the *Seller* workplace.

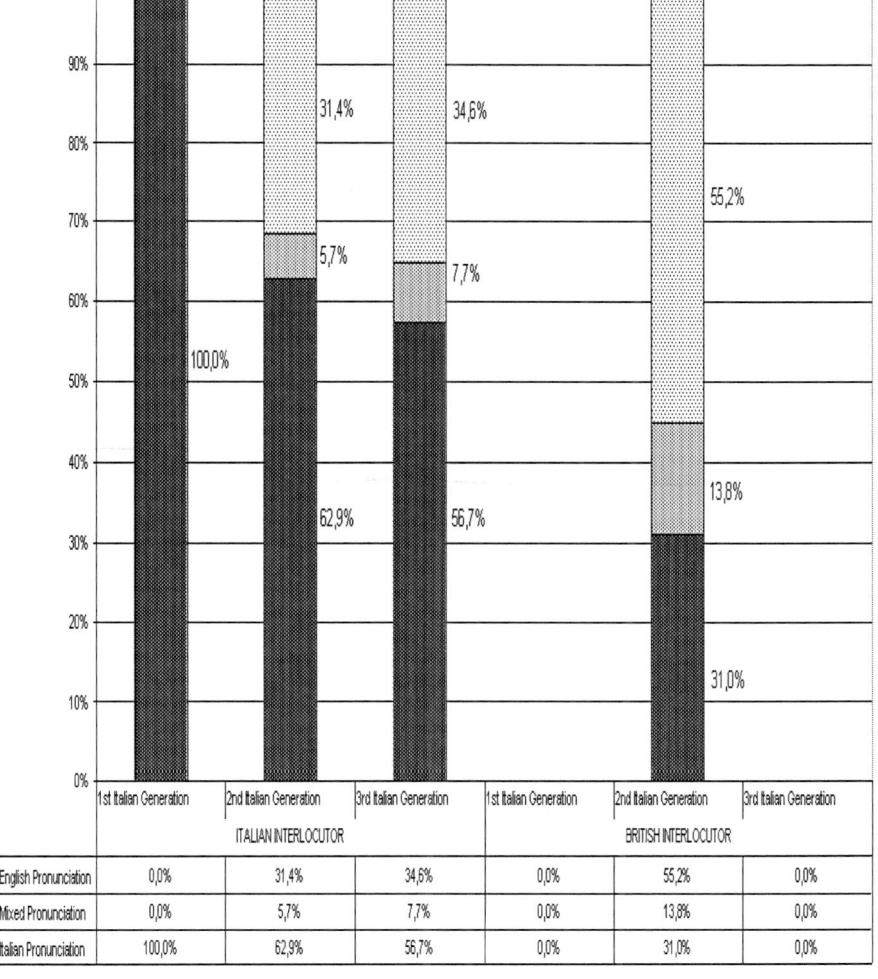

	1st Italian Generation	2nd Italian Generation	3rd Italian Generation	1st Italian Generation	2nd Italian Generation	3rd Italian Generation
		ITALIAN INTERLOCUTOR			BRITISH INTERLOCUTOR	
English Pronunciation	0,0%	31,4%	34,6%	0,0%	55,2%	0,0%
Mixed Pronunciation	0,0%	5,7%	7,7%	0,0%	13,8%	0,0%
Italian Pronunciation	100,0%	62,9%	56,7%	0,0%	31,0%	0,0%

On the other hand, informants in the *Seller* setting may be less motivated to shift depending on the customer's ethnicity because of the different type of business they do. Except for one recording, (see BED04, the market trader Mrs Chirico, whose business exchanges are similar in scope to those of *Restaurants)*, the wholesalers, grouped under the *Seller* label on the other recordings, may not share the same specific purpose. Their talk at work spanned different topics and discourse functions. In the *Seller* workplace, workers are mainly men who spend most of their working day talking to customers, both face-to-face and on the telephone, taking orders, and arranging and taking payments. They also talk to each other, about their private lives as well as their work tasks. Therefore, another possible reason for the findings could be the difference in lexical choice; words used at work are different depending on the workplace in which participants are interacting and this could well influence the level of Anglicisation, or non-Anglicisation, of Italian lexis.

Moving on to my last audience type, the results of Anglicisation of Italian lexis in the *hairdressing* category are interesting. Here the data consist of occurrences from two cohorts only, the 1st and 2nd generation BIs. The *Hairdresser* service encounter proved to be one of the most traditional settings to be analysed and, as a result, it was rare to find all three generations represented there. This is especially true as far as the 3rd generation is concerned as there has been a decline in the trade which has lost popularity over time. The category of hairdressing represents one of the oldest and most traditional trades for Italians abroad and Italian immigrants are often stereotyped as barbers (or restauranteurs) in English language films. When hairdressing was selected as one of the areas of investigation, the expectation was to find this to be the most interesting category, even more than the catering sector, and that it would provide a linguistically rich sample. The fact that 3rd generation BIs are so rarely present in the data, is evidence that the trade is considered old-fashioned and less appealing to young BIs than other career directions. On the other hand, the *Hairdresser* setting proved to be the most suitable type of business for recording the language of 1st generation BIs.

As illustrated in Table 3-11 and Figure 3-5, interesting patterns have emerged regarding the level of Anglicisation of 1st generation speakers where this type of service encounter is concerned. 1st generation informants reveal some degree of Anglicisation (2% to 10.4%), regardless of the interlocutor. Although showing lower levels than 2nd generation informants, the audience design also applies for these speakers in the *Hairdressers* category. On the other hand, in encounters with Italian co-workers or customers, the use of Italian pronunciation (97%) is almost absolute, while the level of Italianisation is slightly lower (86.2%) when interacting with the British.

Table 3-11 Anglicised Italian lexis index of tokens in the *Hairdresser* workplace.

INTERLOCUTOR	ITALIAN			BRITISH		
GENERATION	1st	2nd	3rd	1st	2nd	3rd
ITALIAN PRONUNCIATION	100	10	-	50	-	-
MIXED PRONUNCIATION	1	2	-	2	-	-
ENGLISH PRONUNCIATION	2	11	-	6	2	-
TOTAL	103	23	-	58	2	-

What is more, results concerning the 2nd generation show a different pattern regarding the Anglicisation of Italian lexis in this particular context. When addressing Italian interlocutors, 2nd generation informants are quite balanced in using both Anglicisation (47.8%) and Italianisation (43.5%) of Italian words. However, when the interlocutor is British, the level of Anglicisation increases and an English articulation is preferred (100%). As previously mentioned, the effect that low token numbers can create has to be taken into consideration. Nonetheless, the results are significant in light of the results revealed with Italian interlocutors when the recurrencies of Italian pronunciation were lower than expected.

These patterns are extremely interesting, and the low token numbers are indeed a result of this type of service encounter. Predominantly, the hairdresser/barber business is common only amongst the 1st generation of Italians in the town. Among the three shops in which recording took place, on only one occasion were 2nd generation informants found. In both recordings, BED09 "Tony's" barber shop and BED12, "Giovanni's" hairdresser/barber shop, no 2nd generation informants were present, and only in recording BED11, "Vincenzo's" ladies' and gents' hair salon" were 2nd generation BIs documented. This type of service encounter is representative of the most traditional and typical group of Italians in Bedford. On examination, the results showed that the highest levels of Italian pronunciation were expected in the speech of 1st generation workers in this field, and the lowest levels of Italian pronunciation were expected in the speech of 2nd generation informants. Although findings confirm these expectations, a significant level of Anglicisation was unexpectedly found in the speech of 1st generation BIs (L1 speakers of Italian) when addressing British interlocutors, therefore revealing a degree of accommodation.

Figure 3-5. Anglicised Italian lexis results displayed by percentage in the *Hairdresser* workplace dataset.

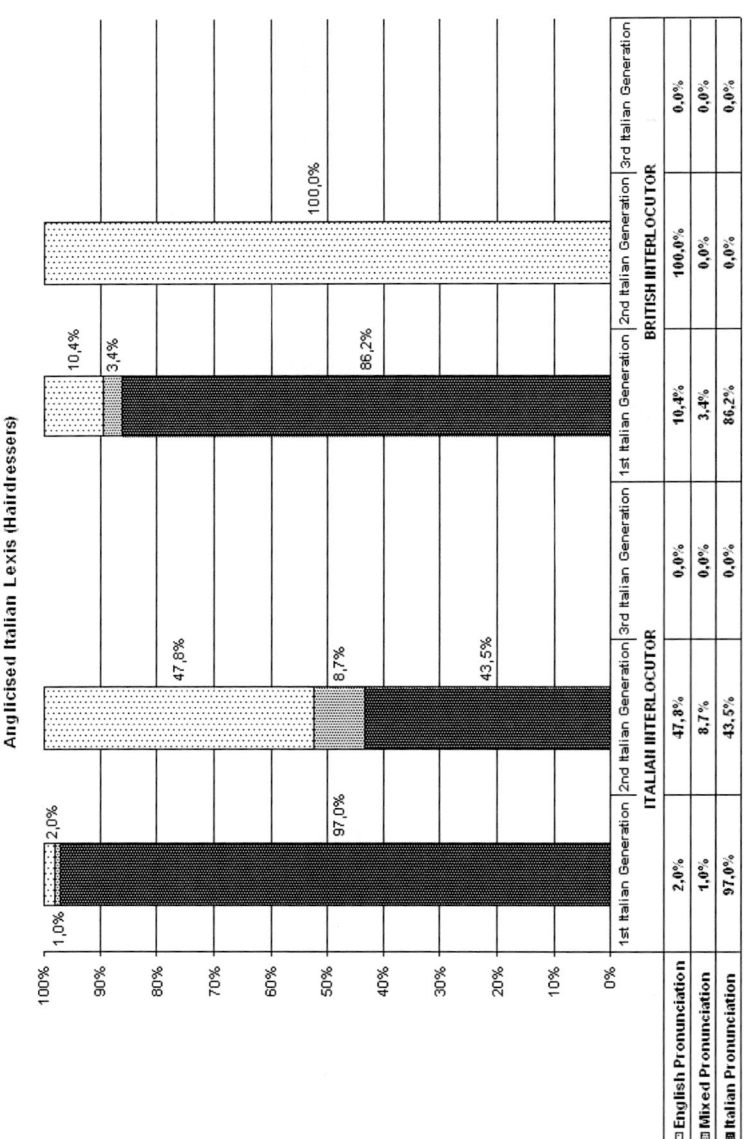

Foool = 1st pen -> strong Italian accent but also strong emphasised features with Ite and Brit

3.5.2 Finding Ib: Foreign /a/

Moving from the comparative and contrastive analysis of the Anglicisation of Italian lexis to the analysis of the other specific phonological features which can favour Anglicisation in the speech of BIs, i.e. the articulation of foreign /a/, the following section shows results according to the workplaces selected.

Table 3-12. Foreign /a/ index of tokens in the *Restaurant* workplace.

INTERLOCUTOR	ITALIAN			BRITISH		
GENERATION	1st	2nd	3rd	1st	2nd	3rd
[a]	26	97	32	-	2	1
[a] / [ɑː]	8	21	34	-	24	2
[æ]	8	3	15	-	-	-
TOTAL	42	121	81	-	26	3

Referring to Boberg's results on foreign (a) nativization in British English, and using them as a starting point, either phoneme /æ/ or /ɑː/ (short /æ/, as in *cat,* and long back /ɑː/, as in *father*) were expected from Bedfordian speakers, mainly when the interlocutor is British, although speakers retaining the original Italian pronunciation were expected to articulate a shorter and fronter /a/ sound (as in the Italian pronunciation of *pasta*), above all when the interlocutor is Italian.

Interpreting the findings *in Restaurants,* we see that the results shown in Table 3-12 and Figure 3-6 confirm the levels of Anglicisation previously discussed. BI informants belonging to the 1st generation produce the phoneme /a/ as it is typically produced in Italian using standard Italian pronunciation (61.9%), when the interlocutor is Italian, although showing a lower percentage than expected. First generation BIs working in the food industry display the lowest levels of Italian articulation if compared to their peers working in the fields of hairdressing and sales. It is interesting to note that the 1st generation in *Restaurants* are more likely to maintain an Italian accent, realizing the foreign (a) as [a], yet a considerable amount of the English phonemes [æ] or [ɑː] (19% each) are found in the articulation of Italian words, such as *margherita, pasta* or *lasagne* for instance, despite the presence of an Italian interlocutor. Maintaining Italian pronunciation would perhaps add prestige in an Italian restaurant setting, and little if any accommodation would be necessary. It would be reasonable to assume that the most common Italian words that have entered into daily use have been

Figure 3-6. Foreign /a/ results displayed by percentage in the *Restaurant* workplace

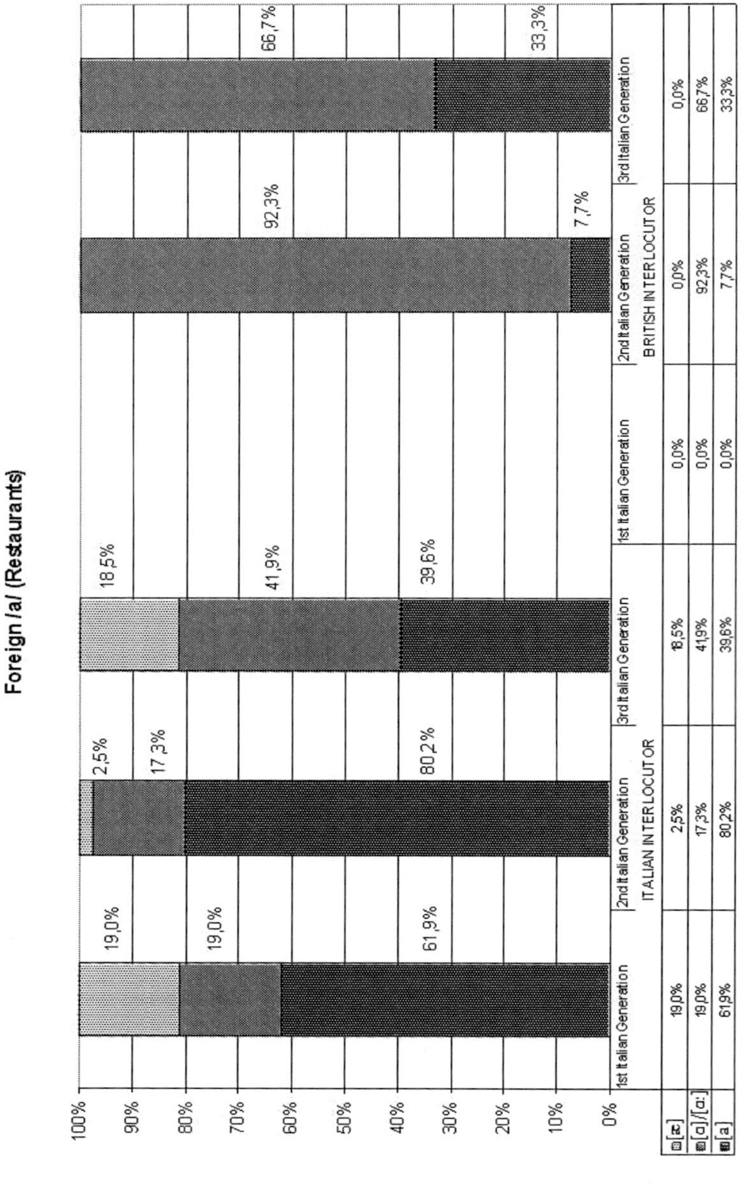

	1st Italian Generation	2nd Italian Generation ITALIAN INTERLOCUTOR	3rd Italian Generation	1st Italian Generation	2nd Italian Generation BRITISH INTERLOCUTOR	3rd Italian Generation
[ɛ]	19,0%	2,5%	18,5%	0,0%	0,0%	0,0%
[ɑ]/[ɑ:]	19,0%	17,3%	41,9%	0,0%	92,3%	66,7%
[a]	61,9%	80,2%	39,6%	0,0%	7,7%	33,3%

accepted with their Anglicised pronunciation and it would be difficult at this stage to return to an authentic Italian pronunciation even if this might appear desirable. Furthermore, 2nd generation BIs in the *Restaurant* workplace show a remarkable shift according to audience design and inter-speaker communication. The highest levels of front and short sound [a] are seen with Italian interlocutors (80.2%), and a British back and long realisation [ɑ:] is seen with Anglo-Bedfordians (92.3%). Again, regarding the Anglicisation of Italian lexis, it seems that compared to other generations of speakers, 2nd generation BIs are keener on a British articulation when the interlocutor is British, as well as markedly realising an Italian phoneme [a] when the interlocutor is Italian.

However, 3rd generation speakers appear to behave differently. Unlike the previous two generations, the younger cohort are the least affected by audience design, and are shown to produce the foreign /a/ as British English phonemes [æ] (18.5%) or [ɑ]/[ɑ:] (41.9%) despite interacting with Italian customers or colleagues. Quite predictably then, when speaking to the British, they are more likely to use a British phoneme (66.7% use of [ɑ]/[ɑ:]) than the Italian variant [a] (33.3%). Again, 3rd generation BIs seem to be affected by different trends, behaving unlike 2nd or 1st generation Italians.

Moving on to the *Seller* results, we immediately see that the most interesting patterns are once again revealed by 3rd generation informants, as shown in Table 3-13 and Figure 3-7.

Table 3-13. Foreign /a/ index of tokens in the *Seller* workplace.

INTERLOCUTOR	ITALIAN			BRITISH		
GENERATION	1st	2nd	3rd	1st	2nd	3rd
[a]	2	97	12	-	7	-
[ɑ] / [ɑ:]	-	37	3	-	10	-
[æ]	-	12	4	-	2	-
TOTAL	2	146	19	-	19	-

Although the 2nd generation displays the highest realisation of Italian [a] (66.4%), what is remarkable is the strong preference for the Italian front phoneme [a] in the speech of 3rd generation informants (63.2%). As I pointed out in the *Restaurant* data above, the 3rd generation of BIs were the least likely to produce the Italian phoneme, whereas in the *Seller* sector the picture changed and younger informants showed a significant preference for the Italian phoneme as far as the articulation of the foreign vowel is concerned. The second most remarkable result is the use of the back allophone [ɑ:] in the speech of 2nd generation BIs with British interlocutors (52.6%). This seems to go against what would be expected from audience design and becomes evident when comparing these results to those *in Restaurants,* where the 2nd generation was the most likely to conform with style-shift, displaying the highest articulation of the British back allophone [ɑ:] (92.3%) when interacting with the British. It seems worthy of note that in the *Seller* service encounters, the same generation of speakers show 36.8% Italian front [a], 52.6% back [ɑ:], and 10.6% [æ].

There is probably a lesser degree of accommodation in the speech of 2nd generation BI sellers. Speakers generally tend to go more or less half-way to meet their interlocutor, whereas in this specific workplace, sellers belonging to 2nd generation BIs do not need to accommodate for any special purpose in their communication. On the other hand, Italian loanwords in the *Restaurant* dataset may be considered as more well-established in English than those in the *Seller* workplace; therefore 2nd generation sellers are less likely to be in a situation where Italian loanwords are used and therefore also less likely to need to display levels of Anglicisation to British interlocutors.

As for the 1st generation of informants, only a small amount of speech was produced by participants in interactions with British non-Italian interlocutors. The informants definitely interact more with Italians and the main trend seems to suggest a very Italianised production of [a].

Lastly, as Table 3-14 and Figure 3-8 display, the *Hairdresser* service encounters confirm a remarkable level of Italianness in the speech of 1st generation informants. Foreign (a) is quite rarely produced as a British [ɑ:] or [æ], and results go against what we might expect from audience design as the informants reveal a significant level of Italian [a] articulation (94.9% and 79.2% respectively) with both Italian and British interlocutors. A slight inter-speaker variation does seem to be present; nonetheless, results show a lower, yet significant, degree of accommodation when the interlocutor is British (20.8% [ɑ:]/[ɑ]). As far as the 2nd generation is concerned, the articulation of foreign /a/ seems to depend on audience design: informants produce [a] in most cases when interacting with Italians (57.1), although quite a significant amount of the back British sound [ɑ:]/[ɑ] emerges (42.9%).

Figure 3-7. Foreign /a/ results displayed by percentage in the *Seller* workplace

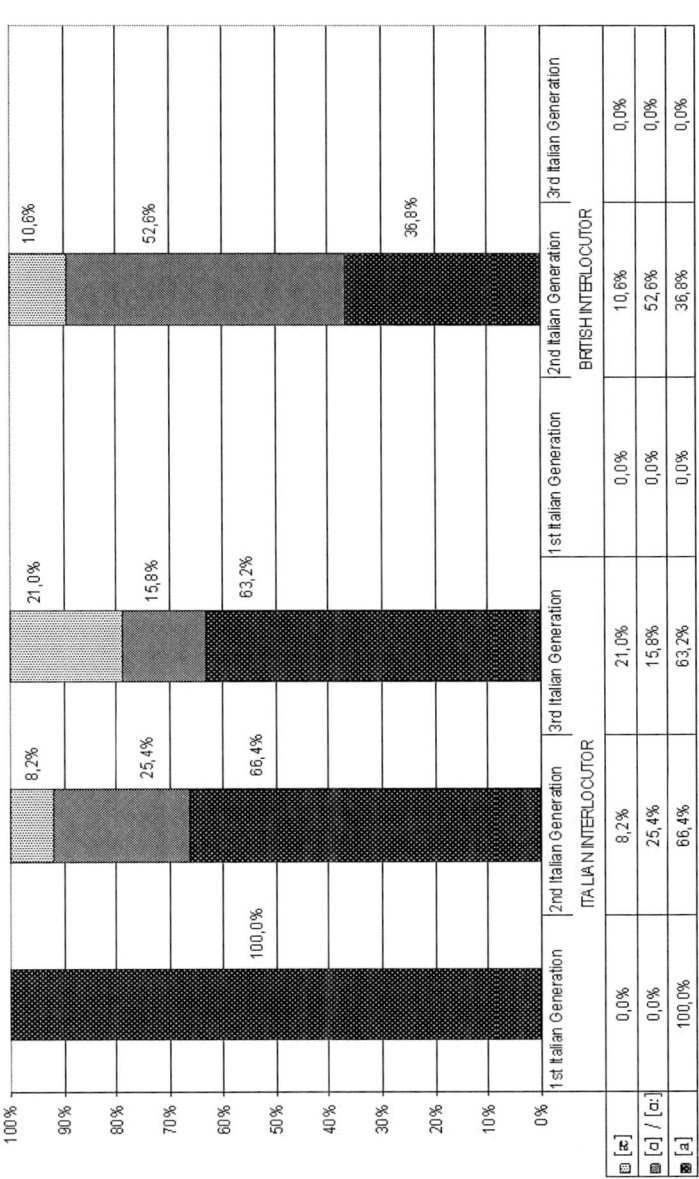

Table 3-14. Foreign /a/ index of tokens in the *Hairdresser* workplace.

INTERLOCUTOR	ITALIAN			BRITISH		
GENERATION	1st	2nd	3rd	1st	2nd	3rd
[a]	55	8	-	19	-	-
[ɑ] / [ɑː]	2	6	-	5	-	-
[æ]	1	-	-	-	-	-
TOTAL	58	14	-	24	-	-

Figure 3-8. Foreign /a/ results displayed by percentage in the *Hairdresser* workplace

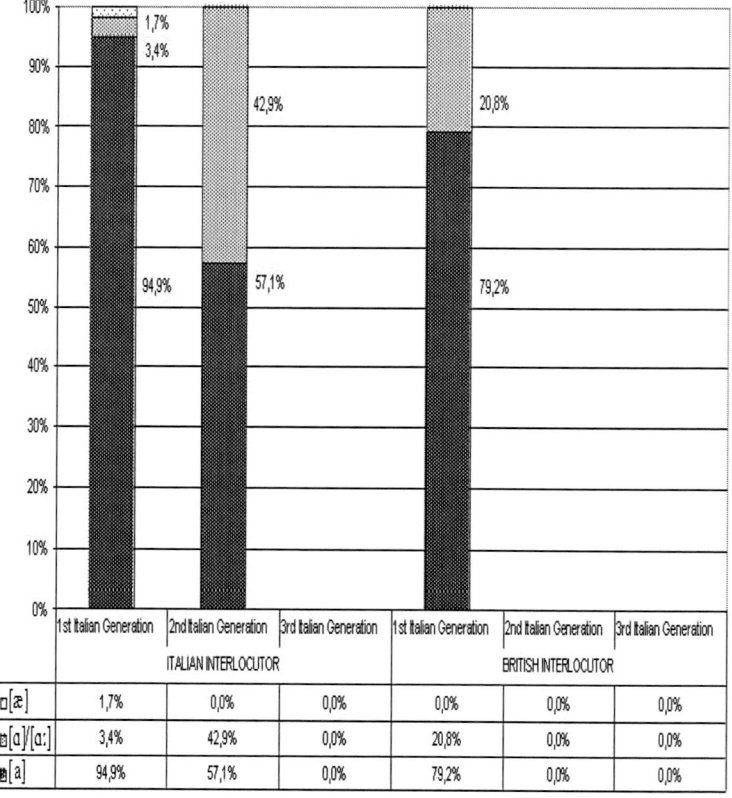

Foreign /a/ (Hairdressers)

	1st Italian Generation	2nd Italian Generation	3rd Italian Generation	1st Italian Generation	2nd Italian Generation	3rd Italian Generation
□[æ]	1,7%	0,0%	0,0%	0,0%	0,0%	0,0%
▣[ɑ]/[ɑː]	3,4%	42,9%	0,0%	20,8%	0,0%	0,0%
▣[a]	94,9%	57,1%	0,0%	79,2%	0,0%	0,0%

Overall, the analysis of the phonological variable brought interesting patterns to light, identifying each generation according to specific trends and characterizing them according to specific features. Each workplace setting also showed remarkable as well as challenging results, and the audience design seemed to work on most occasions.

3.5.3 Finding II: Plurality marking on Italian nouns

"Listen, keep on the pizzes a minute."

Plurality marking on nouns is a feature that is not always correctly used, as previously mentioned, and it was not easy to analyse. Informants produced quite a wide range of variants to the general norm and interesting patterns emerged. In the present work, plurality was approached by taking into consideration the list of tokens already selected for phonological analysis. The main aim was to show whether, and indeed how, English plurality is marked in the speech of the three generations of BIs according to workplace and interlocutor audience design.

Generally, nouns are inflected for grammatical number – i.e., singular or plural by adding a suffix -s to the singular form. As is the case of many foreign nouns adopted in English, including most Italian loanwords, there are exceptions to the –o + es rule, as in the case of *canto,* for instance, where the plural form *is cantos,* and is formed by adding the suffix -s. Apart from spelling rules, not much else has been said about the plurality of foreign nouns. Let us verify how Bedford Italians mark the plurality of Italian lexis in English.

In order to mark variation where it occurred, the results were grouped into three main categories: the first showing occurrences of regular English plurals, the second displaying mixed plurals and the last illustrating plurality marked by Italian grammar rules being applied in a code switched context. The details of the mixed plural category are then represented in tables and figures, where token numbers can be found. The types of plural forms which emerged from the analysis appear to be very distinct (see Table 3-15 for a complete list and illustration of the possible variants found in the corpus).

Table 3-15. Plurality in Anglicised Italian Lexis: list of all variants found in the present corpus.

1. Regular English Plural	E.g. *Two pizzas.*
2. Plural English Number + Italian Singular	E.g. *Two pizza.*
3. Plural English Number + Italian Plural	E.g. *Two pizze.*
4. Plural English Number + Italian Plural + English Plural	E.g. *Two pizzes.*
5. Singular English Number + Italian Plural	E.g. *A pizze.*
6. Singular English Number + Italian Plural + English Plural	E.g. *A pizzes.*
7. Singular Italian Number + Italian Plural + English Plural	E.g. *Una pizzes.*
8. Italian Plural in Code Switched Context	E.g. *Due pizze.*

Assuming these combinations to be the variants which emerged from the utterances of the three generations of BIs, let us verify their distribution in the speech of informants. Among the three workplace settings, *Restaurants* proved to be the most consistent, whereas *Sellers* and *Hairdressers* revealed a lower number of occurrences of irregular deviant forms. According to the findings from *Restaurants,* as in Table 3-16 and Figure 3-9, mixed forms of plurals emerged (60.8%) in the speech of 1st generation BIs when speaking to Italian interlocutors. Nonetheless, some regular patterns are also found (34.8%) and this conforms with the general trend of 1st generation informants in *Restaurants*, as seen for the phonological variable in both contrastive analyses. On the other hand, when interacting with British interlocutors, the informants use mixed plural forms again (100%), although the token number is much lower.

Table 3-16. Plurality in Anglicised Italian Lexis: overall index of tokens in the *Restaurant* workplace.

INTERLOCUTOR	ITALIAN			BRITISH		
GENERATION	1st	2nd	3rd	1st	2nd	3rd
Regular English Plural	8	9	7	-	2	1
Mixed Plural	14	5	6	2	3	-
Italian Plural in Code Switched Context	1	2	1	-	1	-
TOTAL	23	16	14	2	6	1

Analysing the *mixed plural* forms in more detail, as displayed in Table 3-17 and Figure 3-10, the highest usage refers to both plurals showing an English number but an Italian singular (21.7%) and an English number with an Italian plural (21.7%), as in the examples below:

1)   T: […] and *eighteen pizza tropicale.*
2)   T: […] *three pizze* cu l'aglio, come on.

Again, from 1st generation informants in Restaurants, interesting examples of English plural numbers followed by Italian plural nouns and English plurals (17.4%) were found.

3)   T: […] Angela, mo' ci mettiamo ancora *two lasagnes* for Mand. He said he ordered it.

Moving to 2nd generation informants, the highest levels of standardness in plurality (56.2%) were displayed, despite interacting with Italian interlocutors. However, interesting mixed plural forms emerge from their speech (31.3%), showing plurals mainly formed by using an English plural number associated with an Italian singular noun (12.5%), or forming the plural through the pattern Plural English Number + Italian Plural noun + English Plural suffix, as in the following instances:

4)   L: […] *two cappuccino.*
5)   FE: Listen, keep on *the pizzes* a minute.

On the other hand, when 2nd generation informants interact with the British, despite the low token number, results seem to be quite balanced showing that where plurality is concerned, a clear audience design does not apply. Informants make use of regular English plurals (33.3%) as well as displaying a remarkable use of plurals formed by combining plural English numbers, Italian plural nouns and English plural suffix.

6)   SA: […] *two margherites.*

Figure 3-9. Plurality in Anglicised Italian Lexis: overall results displayed by percentage in the *Restaurant* workplace.

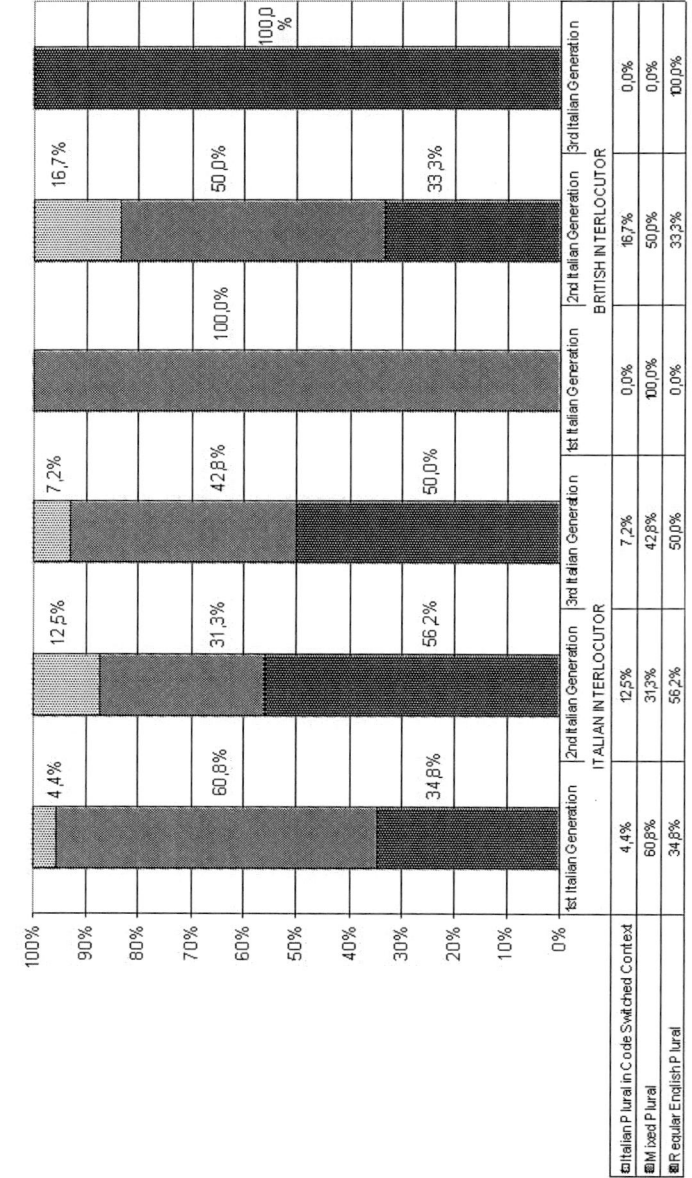

Formation of Plurals in Anglicised Italian Lexis (Restaurants)

	ITALIAN INTERLOCUTOR			BRITISH INTERLOCUTOR		
	1st Italian Generation	2nd Italian Generation	3rd Italian Generation	1st Italian Generation	2nd Italian Generation	3rd Italian Generation
Italian Plural in Code Switched Context	4,4%	12,5%	7,2%	0,0%	16,7%	0,0%
Mixed Plural	60,8%	31,3%	42,8%	100,0%	50,0%	0,0%
Regular English Plural	34,8%	56,2%	50,0%	0,0%	33,3%	100,0%

Informants of the 3rd generation proved to be the most consistent when forming plurals both with Italians (50%) and non-Italians (100%). Nonetheless, there are cases of interesting examples of plurals formed by the English pattern number followed by the Italian plural noun (21.4%) as in example n° 7, and the English number followed by the Italian plural noun and English plural suffix (21.4%) as in n° 8.

7)   FA: Angela, *two lasagne* and one single please.
8)   UIM[15]: Salad take away? Angelita, two *lasagnes* please.

Table 3-17. Plurality in Anglicised Italian Lexis: detailed index of tokens for each occurrence in the *Restaurant* workplace.

INTERLOCUTOR	ITALIAN			BRITISH		
GENERATION	1st	2nd	3rd	1st	2nd	3rd
Regular English Plural	8	9	7	-	2	1
Plural English Number + Italian Singular	5	2	-	2	-	-
Plural English Number + Italian Plural	5	-	3	-	-	-
Plural English Number + It. Pl. + En. Pl.	4	2	3	-	3	-
Singular English Number + Italian Plural	-	1	-	-	-	-
Singular English Number + It.Pl. + En.Pl	-	-	-	-	-	-
Singular Italian Number + It. Pl. + En. Pl.	-	-	-	-	-	-
Italian Plural in Code Switched Context	1	2	1	-	1	-
TOTAL	23	16	14	2	6	1

---

[15] Informants are identified by initials or first name when given, for reasons of anonymity. Specifically in this case, FA stands for FiorAngelo, while UIM stands for "Unknown Italian Male".

Figure 3-10. Plurality in Anglicised Italian Lexis: detailed index of tokens for each occurrence in the *Restaurant* workplace.

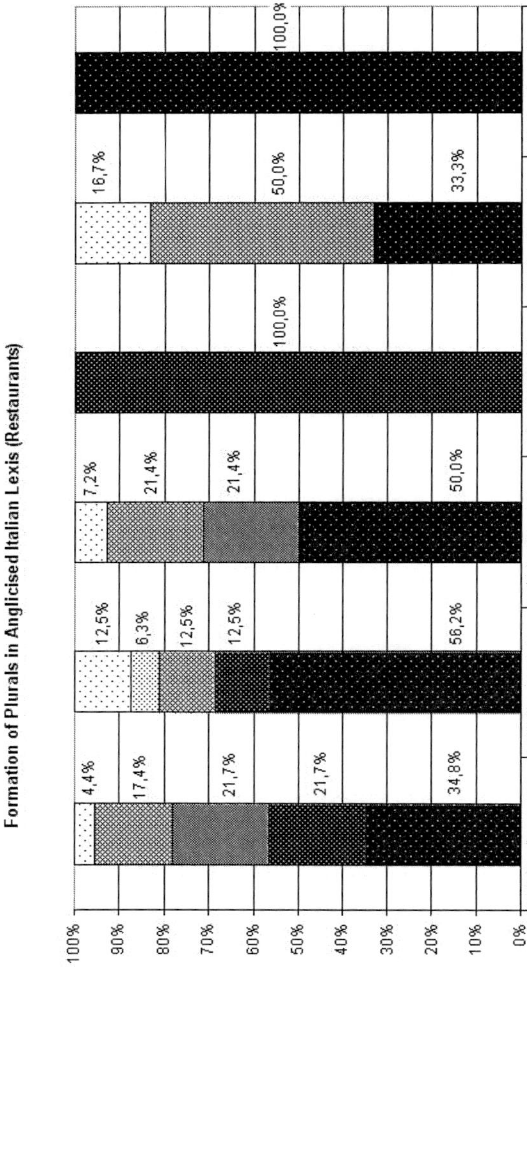

Formation of Plurals in Anglicised Italian Lexis (Restaurants)

	ITALIAN INTERLOCUTOR			BRITISH INTERLOCUTOR		
	1st Italian Generation	2nd Italian Generation	3rd Italian Generation	1st Italian Generation	2nd Italian Generation	3rd Italian Generation
Italian Plural in Code Switched Context	4,4%	12,5%	7,2%	0,0%	16,7%	0,0%
Singular Italian Number + It. Pl. + En. Pl.	0,0%	0,0%	0,0%	0,0%	0,0%	0,0%
Singular English Number + It.Pl. + En.Pl	0,0%	0,0%	0,0%	0,0%	0,0%	0,0%
Singular English Number + Italian Plural	0,0%	6,3%	0,0%	0,0%	0,0%	0,0%
Plural English Number + It. Pl. + En. Pl.	17,4%	12,5%	21,4%	0,0%	50,0%	0,0%
Plural English Number + Italian Plural	21,7%	0,0%	21,4%	0,0%	0,0%	0,0%
Plural English Number + Italian Singular	21,7%	12,5%	0,0%	100,0%	0,0%	0,0%
Regular English Plural	34,8%	56,2%	50,0%	0,0%	33,3%	100,0%

On examination of the *Seller* workplace, results brought to light occurrences of plural formation in the speech of 2nd generation BIs only. No occurrences were found in the conversations and business encounters of either 1st or 3rd generation informants. As Table 3-18 and Figure 3-11 present, the distribution of tokens shows a significant degree of accommodation and a trend towards the use of non-standard plurality in their speech.

Table 3-18. Plurality in Anglicised Italian Lexis: overall index of tokens in the *Seller* workplace.

INTERLOCUTOR	ITALIAN			BRITISH		
GENERATION	1st	2nd	3rd	1st	2nd	3rd
Regular English Plural	-	2	-	-	3	-
Mixed Plural	-	4	-	-	3	-
Italian Plural in Code Switched Context	-	-	-	-	1	-
TOTAL	-	6	-	-	7	-

Overall, 2nd generation informants display a wide range of mixed plurals and a consistent level of Italian influence over plural formation (66.7%) when communicating with Italian interlocutors, therefore confirming the degree of accommodation to their audience. On the other hand, when the interlocutor is British, 2nd generation informants seem to shift to English standard patterns (42.8%), while also showing instances of mixed plural forms (42.9%).The results appear quite balanced.

Let us verify in more detail what the 2nd generation BIs' preferences are as far as the plurality of Italian nouns is concerned. As Table 3-19 and Figure 3-12 display, the preferred pattern consists of forming plurals by adding an Italian plural noun to a form that is semantically marked as plural in the English (33.3%), as in the following example.

9) IFC[16]: We want *some cappuccini* and some of those.

The Italian plural noun *cappuccini* is preferred to a regular English plural *cappuccinos,* even though it is in a complete English sentence structure.

---

[16] Please note the acronym IFC stands for Italian Female Customer.

Figure 3-11. Plurality in Anglicised Italian Lexis: overall results displayed by percentage in the *Seller* workplace

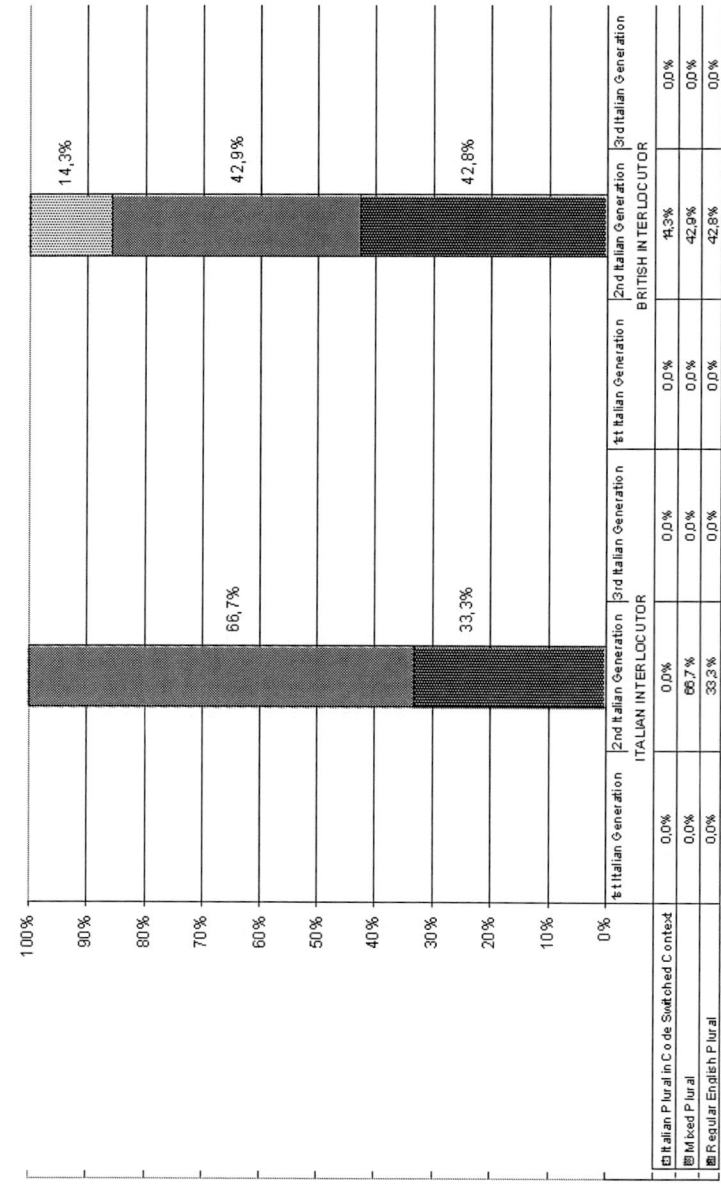

Another pattern which is worth mentioning is the formation of plurals through the use of a plural number associated with an Italian singular noun (16.7%), such as:

10) S: [...] *two kilo pasta secca*, [...]

In place of a regular plural *two kilos (of) pastas (secca)*; or through the pattern singular English number followed by an Italian plural noun (16.7%), as in:

11) S: ok? That's everything, all right? Ok, *one kilo confetti*, [...]

It is worth noting that *one kilo confetti* is preferred to *one kilo of confettos* (or sugar almonds). This is a very interesting plural formation, above all considering that the plural form '*confetti*' exists in the English language albeit with a different meaning i.e. the tiny pieces of coloured paper scattered during festive occasions.

Table 3-19. Plurality in Anglicised Italian Lexis: detailed index of tokens for each occurrence in the *Seller* workplace.

INTERLOCUTOR	ITALIAN			BRITISH		
GENERATION	1st	2nd	3rd	1st	2nd	3rd
Regular English Plural	-	2	-	-	3	-
Plural English Number + Italian Singular	-	1	-	-	-	-
Plural English Number + Italian Plural	-	2	-	-	-	-
Plural English Number + It. Pl. + En. Pl.	-	-	-	-	-	-
Singular English Number + Italian Plural	-	1	-	-	1	-
Singular English Number + It.Pl. + En.Pl	-	-	-	-	1	-
Singular Italian Number + It. Pl.+ En. Pl.	-	-	-	-	1	-
Italian Plural in Code Switched Context	-	-	-	-	1	-
TOTAL	-	6	-	-	7	-

As for the interaction with British interlocutors, detailed occurrences showed some interesting plurals too. In spite of a significant amount of regular English plurals (42.8%), some examples of other mixed plurals are worthy of note.

The most remarkable and challenging issue is the plurality found in the use of singular English number plus an Italian noun and English plural suffix (14.3%), or singular Italian number followed by an Italian plural noun and an English plural suffix (14.3%), as exemplified below:

Figure 3-12. Plurality in Anglicised Italian Lexis: detailed index of tokens for each occurrence in the *Seller* workplace

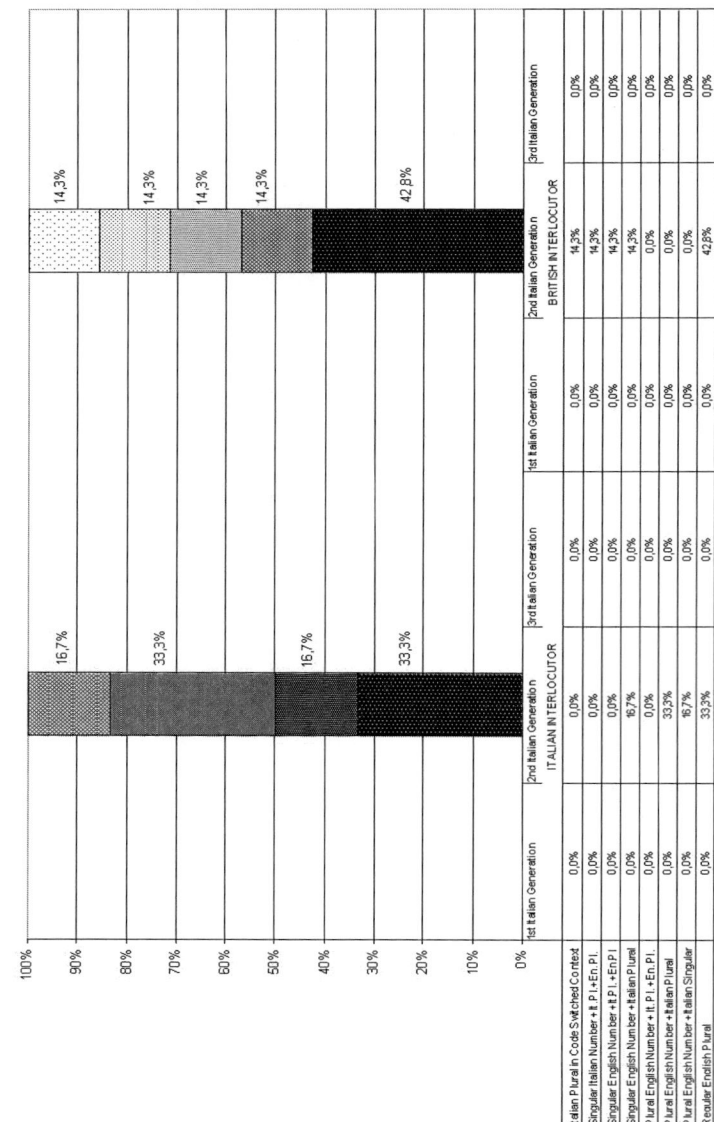

12)   SM: Anything else? *A rosettes*[17]?
13)   SM: [...] *Tre crocchelles*?

In the last two examples, 2nd generation *Seller* informants formed plurals in various ways. The different usages amongst informants, show significant patterns even though they are only supported by low token numbers. These findings require further investigation and new data collection with a higher number of occurrences in order to verify whether or not these patterns become a stable feature of BI English in future.

Nonetheless, these patterns represent a first attempt to throw light on one aspect of the morphology of BIs as far as a non standard feature is concerned.

Lastly, considering the results of the third workplace, the *Hairdressers*, we see from Tables 3-20 and 3-21, and Figures 3-13 and 3-14 that only a general trend can be assumed regarding the two generations of informants represented here. Nonetheless, if we compare the three workplaces, something interesting emerges as far as the plurality of Anglicised Italian lexis is concerned.

Table 3-20. Plurality in Anglicised Italian Lexis: detailed index of tokens for each occurrence in the *Hairdresser* workplace.

INTERLOCUTOR	ITALIAN			BRITISH		
GENERATION	1st	2nd	3rd	1st	2nd	3rd
Regular English Plural	1	1	-	-	-	-
Mixed Plural	-	-	-	-	-	-
Italian Plural in Code Switched Context	1	-	-	-	-	-
TOTAL	2	1	-	-	-	-

---

[17] The Italian nouns *rosetta* (pl. *rosette*) and *crocchella* (pl. *crocchelle*) are types of bread. The first is a rose cut roll, while the latter is a type of crisp loaf.

Table 3-21. Plurality in Anglicised Italian Lexis: overall index of tokens in the _Hairdresser_ workplace.

INTERLOCUTOR	ITALIAN			BRITISH		
GENERATION	1st	2nd	3rd	1st	2nd	3rd
Regular English Plural	1	1	-	-	-	-
Plural English Number + Italian Singular	-	-	-	-	-	-
Plural English Number + Italian Plural	-	-	-	-	-	-
Plural English Number + It. Pl. + En. Pl.	-	-	-	-	-	-
Singular English Number + Italian Plural	-	-	-	-	-	-
Singular English Number + It.Pl. + En.Pl	-	-	-	-	-	-
Singular Italian Number + It. Pl.+ En. Pl.	-	-	-	-	-	-
Italian Plural in Code Switched Context	1	-	-	-	-	-
TOTAL	2	1	-	-	-	-

The 1st generation of informants who represent the _Hairdressers_ in the present corpus are quite inconsistent in the number of occurrences of plural Italian nouns used. However, as expected, the trend is clear. First generation informants interacting with Italians, either use regular English plural forms (50%) or Italian plurals in a code switched context (50%) as in the example below:

14) R: Ah, ah, dici _i stick italiani_?

Using an English noun, _stick,_ followed by an Italian plural, _italiani,_ in a code-switched conversation.

Due to the type of business exchanges they have, conforming with the results I found in the phonology, this generation of informants either speak English with a high level of occurrences of Italian articulation, or Italian, sometimes code switched with English. On the other hand, the type of business requires a different lexical choice compared to that examined in the workplaces of _Restaurants_ and _Sellers_, a reason why less occurrences of plurality emerged.

Figure 3-13. Plurality in Anglicised Italian Lexis: detailed index of tokens for each occurrence in the *Hairdresser* workplace

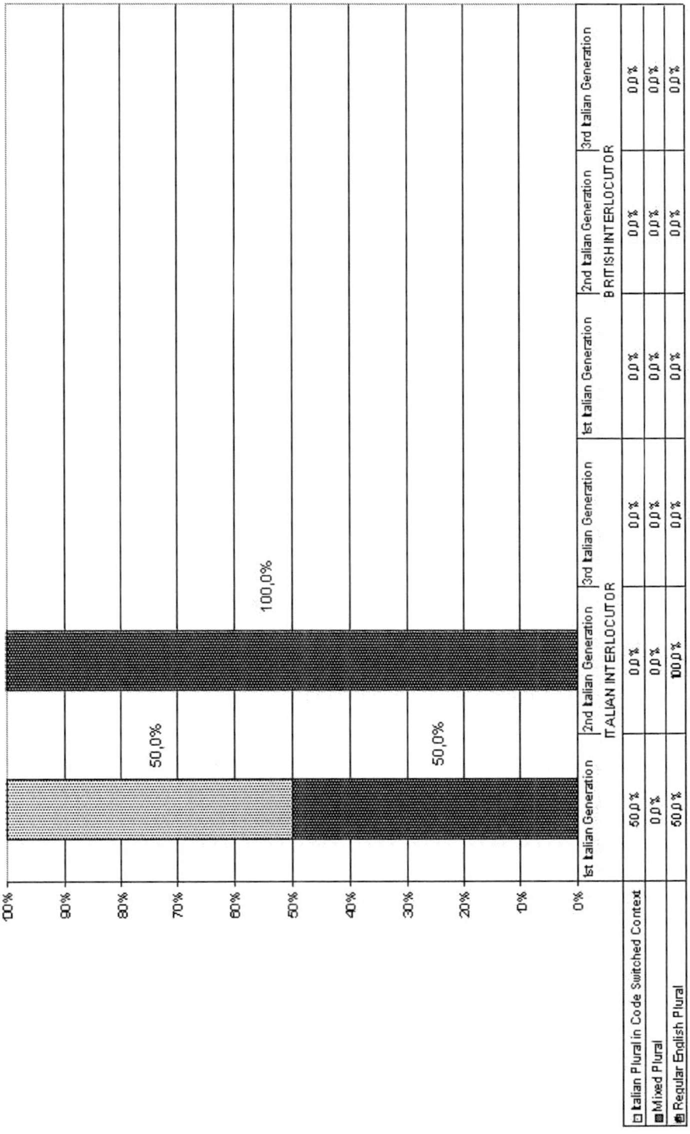
Formation of Plurals in Anglicised Italian Lexis (Hairdressers)
100%
90%
80%
70%
60%
50%
40%
30%
20%
10%
0%
50,0%
50,0%
100,0%
1st Italian Generation
2nd Italian Generation
3rd Italian Generation
ITALIAN INTERLOCUTOR
1st Italian Generation
2nd Italian Generation
3rd Italian Generation
BRITISH INTERLOCUTOR
Italian Plural in Code Switched Context 50,0% 0,0% 0,0% 0,0% 0,0% 0,0%
Mixed Plural 0,0% 0,0% 0,0% 0,0% 0,0% 0,0%
Regular English Plural 50,0% 100,0% 0,0% 0,0% 0,0% 0,0%

Figure 3-14. Plurality in Anglicised Italian Lexis: detailed index of tokens for each occurrence in the *Hairdresser* workplace

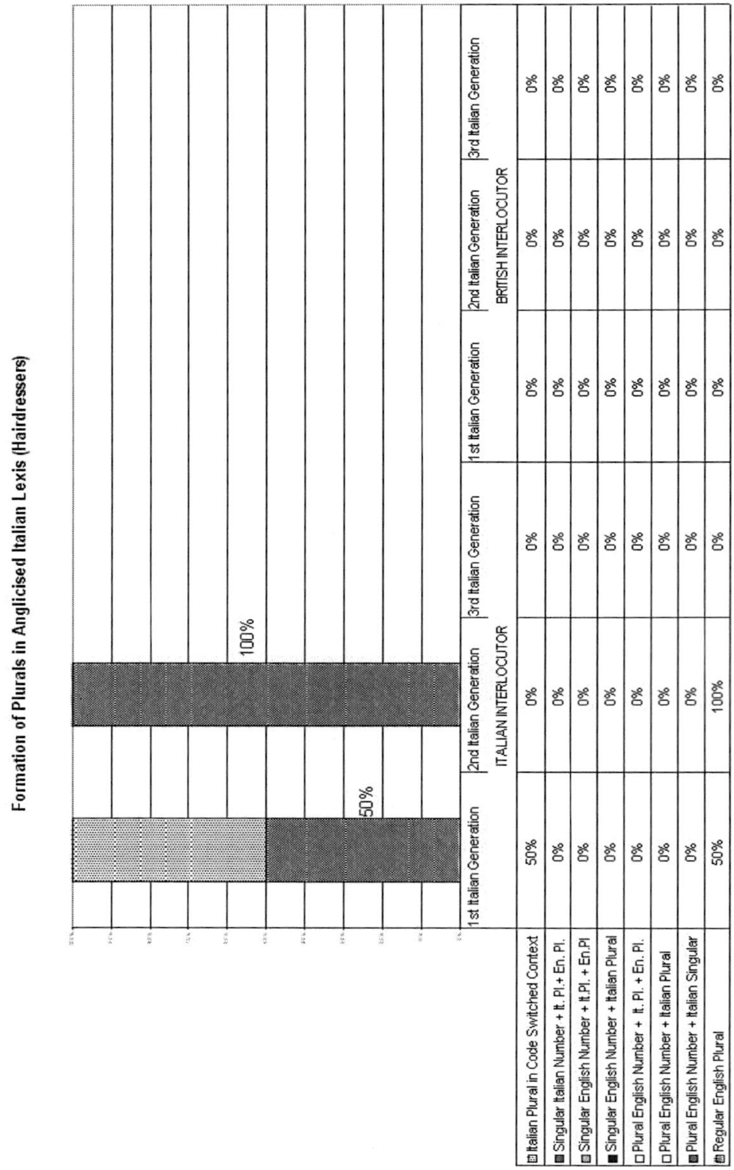

Formation of Plurals in Anglicised Italian Lexis (Hairdressers)

	ITALIAN INTERLOCUTOR			BRITISH INTERLOCUTOR		
	1st Italian Generation	2nd Italian Generation	3rd Italian Generation	1st Italian Generation	2nd Italian Generation	3rd Italian Generation
Italian Plural in Code Switched Context	50%	0%	0%	0%	0%	0%
Singular Italian Number + It. Pl.+ En. Pl.	0%	0%	0%	0%	0%	0%
Singular English Number + It.Pl. + En.Pl	0%	0%	0%	0%	0%	0%
Singular English Number + Italian Plural	0%	0%	0%	0%	0%	0%
Plural English Number + It. Pl. + En. Pl.	0%	0%	0%	0%	0%	0%
Plural English Number + Italian Plural	0%	0%	0%	0%	0%	0%
Plural English Number + Italian Singular	0%	100%	0%	0%	0%	0%
Regular English Plural	50%	100%	0%	0%	0%	0%

3.5.4 Finding III: Presence/absence of inversion in question formation

"When you're gonna see her again?"

As far as the presence/absence of inversion in question formation is concerned, I started from the general assumptions concerning the AUX- and WH-question structures of standard English, for which the most common question structures are: Main Verb + Subject as in *Was the book heavy?*, (Question word +) Auxiliary Verb + Object or Main Verb, as in *(When) is the train leaving?* for object questions, and Question word + Main Verb + Subject, as in *Who lives in that house?* for subject questions.

Investigating different instances of the presence/absence of inversion in question formation in the speech of the three generations of BIs, with respect to the selected workplaces and the ethnicity of interlocutors, interesting patterns resulted, particularly from wh-question formation. In rating the results, findings were grouped into three main question categories: Standard Inverted (e.g. Do you want a coffee?) Standard Non-Inverted (e.g. You got any mustard?), and Non-Standard (e.g. What they'll do?), in which non-inversion errors occurred.

As Table 3-22 and Figure 3-15 show, the distribution of the present feature across the three generations, with regard to Italian versus British interlocutors, appears interesting.

Table 3-22. Presence/absence of inversion in BI question formation: detailed index of tokens for each occurrence in the *Restaurant* workplace.

INTERLOCUTOR	ITALIAN			BRITISH		
GENERATION	1st	2nd	3rd	1st	2nd	3rd
Standard Inverted	1	53	42	1	29	8
Standard Non-Inverted	3	18	22	-	-	2
Non-standard	1	8	3	-	1	1
TOTAL	5	79	67	1	30	11

It is worth paying attention to the levels of non-standardness. Overall, the three generations of the *Restaurant* data seem to be very standard if we consider the levels of standard inverted as well as standard non-inverted questions. Yet surprisingly, some non-standard occurrences in question structures that a British English speaker would not usually form come to light. Let us see some examples taken from the interactions with Italian interlocutors, with reference to each of the three generations respectively.

1)   T: What you like best the ice-cream then?
2)   L: And then what they'll do?
3)   EN: Ah, Anna, what else we've got free?

In these occurrences, all three generations show questions formed in a non-standard way not normally adopted by British English speakers. Generally speaking, levels of non-standardness are not so consistent as to allow the claim that there is an ongoing variation in this feature of the BIs' morphology, but there are definitely signs that we should be monitoring to verify whether this feature is going towards a non-standard stabilisation.

First generation BIs seem to form their wh-questions non-inverting subject and auxiliary (29%) more than 2nd and 3rd generation informants (10.1% and 4.5% respectively); nonetheless, they all seem quite balanced. Audience design applies less in the analysis of this feature, but it is worth paying attention to the results 3rd generation speakers display when interacting with the British (9.1%) versus 2nd generation informants (3.3%). This result seems to conform with previous research studies about 3rd generation BIs (Guzzo 2007; Guzzo, Fox, Britain forthcoming) who displayed increasing levels of non-Britishness in both their identity perception and phonology. 3rd generation behaviour is interesting and shows the use of more non-standard forms with British interlocutors than with Italians. They accommodate less to the British in both their morphology and phonology than their parents, which could be a reflection of their chosen identity perception as non-British.

Figure 3-15. Presence/absence of inversion in BI question formation: detailed index of tokens for each occurrence in the *Restaurant* workplace

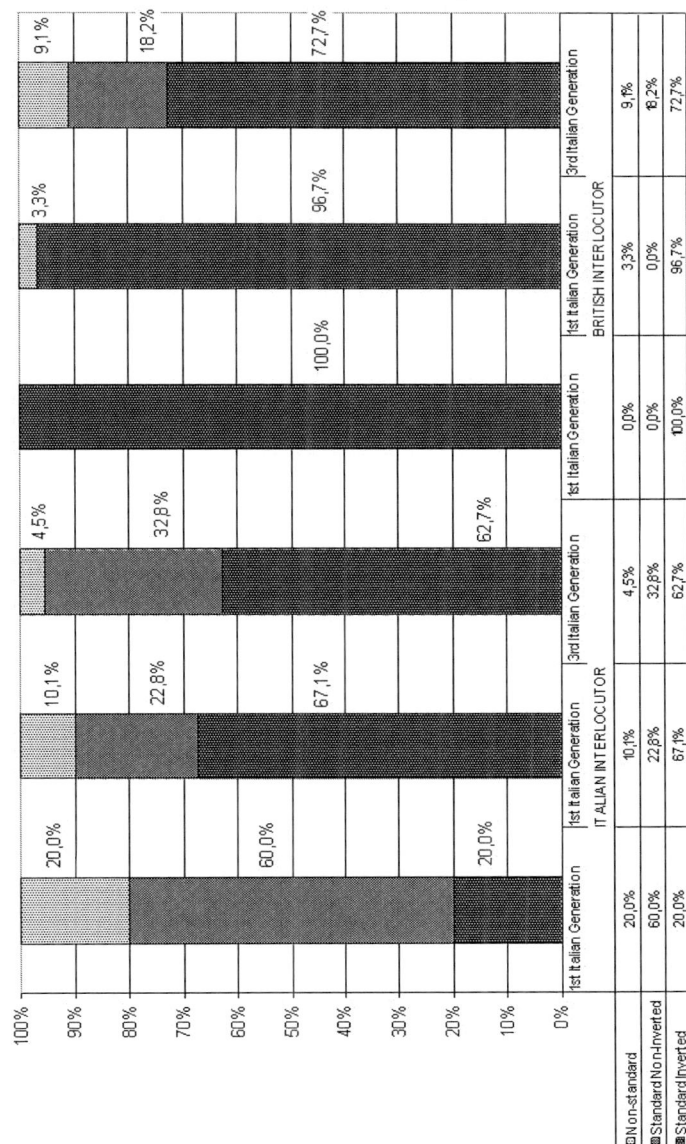

Moving to the *Seller* data set, as shown in Table 3-23 and Figure 3-16, the most interesting results are those referring to 3rd generation informants interacting with Italians, which seem higher (16.1%) than the ones found in the *Restaurant* set (4.5%).

Table 3-23. Presence/absence of inversion in BI question formation: detailed index of tokens for each occurrence in the *Seller* workplace.

INTERLOCUTOR	ITALIAN			BRITISH		
GENERATION	1st	2nd	3rd	1st	2nd	3rd
Standard Inverted	-	75	19	-	48	2
Standard Non-Inverted	-	22	7	-	8	1
Non-standard	1	10	5	-	1	-
TOTAL	1	107	31	-	57	3

According to the analysis of question formation, 3rd generation informants recorded in the *Seller* set reveal a more consistent level of accommodation towards the interlocutor type. Some examples of question formation follow.

4) G^{18}: Why you just buy these?
5)   G: Why Sab you haven't got a copy of it?
6)   DE: Well, why they care about?

Despite being very regular most of the time with both standard inverted (61.3%) and standard non-inverted questions (22.6%), when forming a wh-question, 3rd generation informants of the *Seller* dataset do not invert subject-auxiliary making the question formation non-standard.

Interestingly, 2nd generation informants, on the other hand, seem to show patterns quite close to those in the *Restaurant* data set. Over a total number of 107 occurrences of questions, although at a much lower frequency (9.3%), informants display interesting non-standard forms, as in the following examples:

---

[18] Informant G, i.e. Giuseppe, was first recorded in 2004 (Guzzo 2005, 2007) when he was just seventeen years old and more recently for this study. A comparative analysis in future with the same informant would be interesting in order to verify whether further examples of parallel linguistic behaviour can be found.

7)   SM: When you're gonna see her again?
8)   IFC1: How much it can weight?

Furthermore, when interacting with a British interlocutor, both generations show a significant degree of accommodation and the lowest occurrences of non-standard forms (1.7% for 2nd generation and 0% for 3rd generation). Here is an example taken from the dataset:

9)   AN: How many single cream you order for tomorrow?

Overall, audience design with regard to the ethnicity of the interlocutors does have an effect over the level of morphological variation.

Last but not least, the *Hairdresser* dataset confirms that the highest levels of non-standardness, as far as question formation is concerned, are to be found in 1st generation BIs working in this more traditional workplace. As Table 3-24 and Figure 3-17 present, the usage of non-standard question forms is very balanced for both types of interlocutors. Audience design seems not to apply when referring to 1st generation informants in this specific workplace. More probably, they have not developed enough strategic communication skills in English as they are L1 speakers of Italian. By contrast, 2nd generation informants show more regular patterns.

Figure 3-16. Presence/absence of inversion in BI question formation: detailed index of tokens for each occurrence in the *Seller* workplace

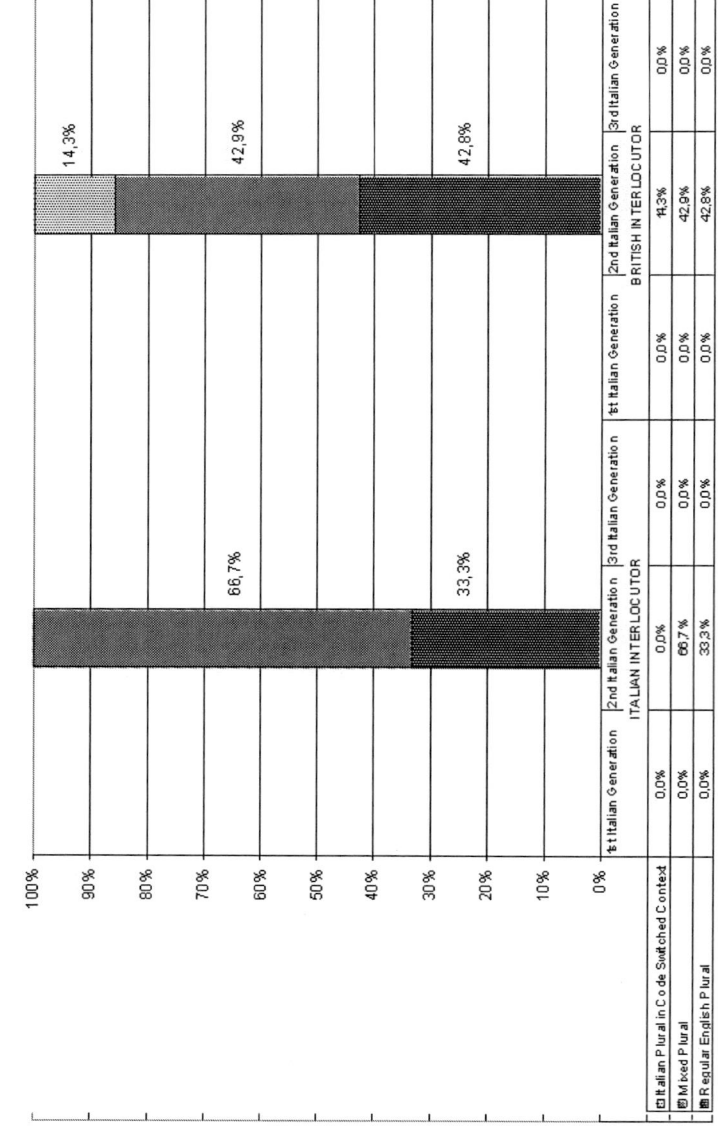

Table 3-24. Presence/absence of inversion in BI question formation: detailed index of tokens for each occurrence in the *Hairdresser* workplace dataset.

INTERLOCUTOR	ITALIAN			BRITISH		
GENERATION	1st	2nd	3rd	1st	2nd	3rd
Standard Inverted	15	12	-	20	2	1
Standard Non-Inverted	39	3	-	19	-	-
Non-standard	17	-	-	12	-	-
TOTAL	71	15	-	51	3	1

As can be seen in the table above, 1st generation BIs use a consistent amount of non-standard question formation in their speech with Italians (23.9%) as well as a similar level of use with the British (23.5%). As we can see from one of the examples taken from an interaction with British interlocutors, they show non-standard simple non-inverted questions apart from wh-questions. The type of L2 errors are more complex in the speech of 1st generation *Hairdressers*. Some examples follow below:

10) V: You know how much costs that?
11) V: When you come Pasquà?
12) GI: Italian police what they say?

Figure 3-17. Presence/absence of inversion in BI question formation: detailed index of tokens for each occurrence in the *Hairdresser* workplace dataset

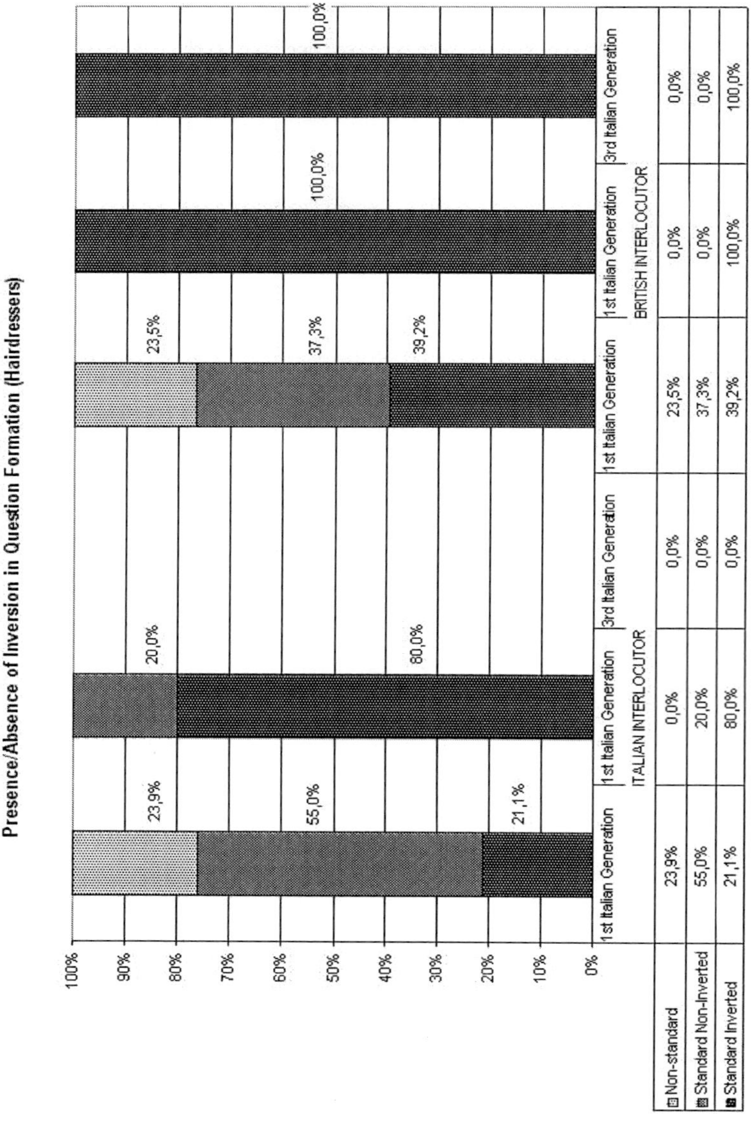

In the above examples extracted from service encounters with Italian interlocutors, 1st generation informants reveal very interesting patterns. In order to convey the idea of a question, they seem to use an Italian question structure, and question intonation. More evident than in the other examples shown above, those referring to this dataset are the most significant, regarding the Italian structure the informants adopted. Errors are not only in the non-inverted wh- or AUX- questions, but in the whole structure, which is non-standard.

Furthermore, as mentioned above, the speakers do not use different amounts of non-standard patterns with different interlocutors. See the examples below:

13) TO: So, wha- wha- wha- what he think?
14) TO: So, when you're gonna go back to spend with that car?

In all the present extracts, informants address British interlocutors, yet their questions show not only non-inversion, but other L2 errors, such as 3rd person present tense –s absence, as in example 13. Moreover, the meaning is not easily understood, as in the example 14, and the question style is convoluted and vague.

3.5.5 Finding IV: Presence/absence of third person zero verbal person marking

"As soon as that cook, I can give you one."

The third morphological variable concerns the presence or absence of third person present tense –s which is generally associated with the third person singular as opposed to the non-singular categories. Although previous research on this feature has concentrated on "classroom language testing" aimed at finding errors in the acquisition of English as L2, as mentioned in previous paragraphs, no research has taken naturally occurring language into consideration. Given that person markers typically combine person distinctions with those of number, a list of BI tokens of present-tense verbal –s exhibits number distinction with regard to the third person.

As Table 3-25 and Figure 3-18 display, results for speakers recorded in the *Restaurant* dataset seem to be quite clear. Surprisingly, 3rd generation speech is marked by higher non-usage of third person –s (26.3%) than that of the 2nd generation (3.7%), which barely shows errors. Although both seem to widely use standard verbal person marking with both Italian and

British interlocutors, the level of zero –s in the speech of 3rd generation informants is striking.

Table 3-25. Presence/absence of third person zero verbal person marking: detailed index of tokens for each occurrence in the *Restaurant* workplace dataset.

INTERLOCUTOR	ITALIAN			BRITISH		
GENERATION	1st	2nd	3rd	1st	2nd	3rd
+S	-	26	14	-	2	1
-S	-	1	5	-	-	-
TOTAL	-	27	19	-	2	1

Let us read some examples taken from the transcription of the recordings with regard to 3rd generation BIs.

15) EN: As soon as *that cook*, I can give you one.
16) IM1: *Face look* nice.
17) IM1: Let's see what *one want* for desert now, yeah?

Levels of 3rd person present tense –s absence confirm the distance between 3rd generation BIs and the generation of their parents. Again 3rd generation speakers seem to behave unlike 2nd generation BIs.

Figure 3-18. Presence/absence of third person zero verbal person marking: detailed index of tokens for each occurrence in the *Restaurant* workplace dataset

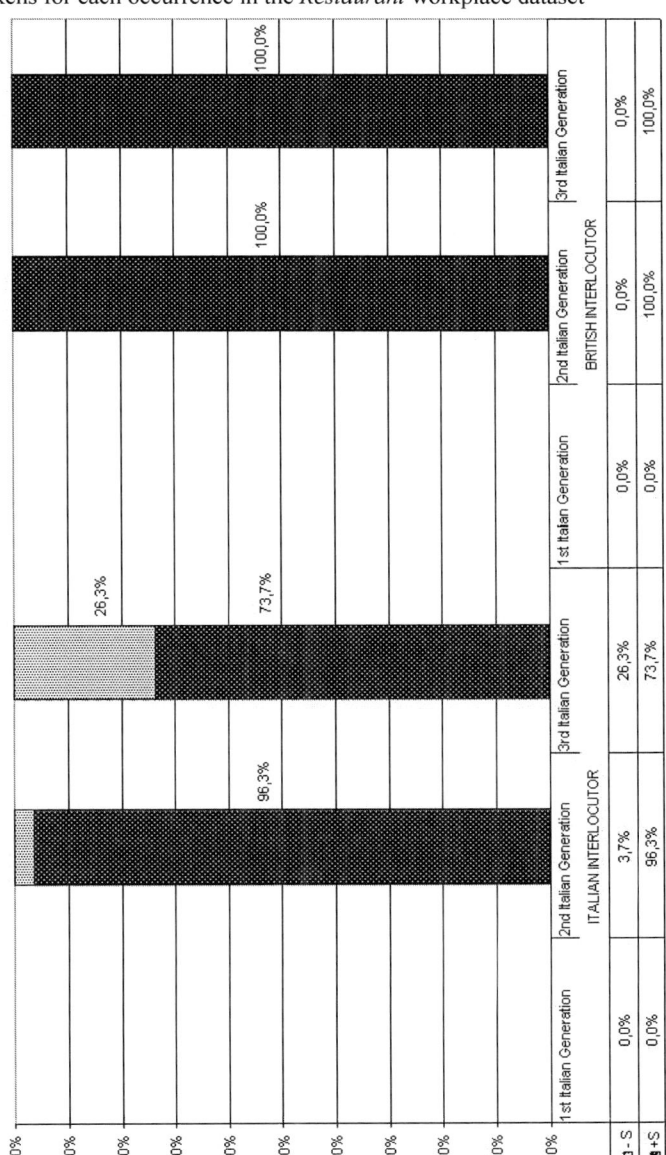

Although this trend seems to be quite consistent and confirmed in the findings from the *Seller* dataset, explanations are only sketchy. It might be interesting to investigate this feature further in a wider range of datasets so as to verify whether there is evidence of a steady trend towards zero marking or not. Thus far I can assume it is a transfer from L1. Given the differences with the 2nd generation, it could be considered as an error influenced by L1 in the 1st generation's speech, but this explanation is quite unlikely regarding the speech of 3rd generation BIs. Arguably, I would suggest this result could be a reflection of the 3rd generation's non-Britishness, rather than a reflection of Italian-ness, and that it is used as a way of asserting their cultural identity as non-British through the absence of features which are typical of standard British English. This could also be true for some of the other findings illustrated previously with regard to 3rd generation informants. Moreover, this would find confirmation in the results of a multicultural international project which investigated change in phonological hiatus resolution marking, and compared data from three ethnic groups: the British, the Bangladeshi and the Italians (Britain, Fox & Guzzo, forthcoming). There seems to be change afoot in the language of this generation of BIs and the direction is towards the minority ethnic form of English.

Moving to the *Seller* dataset, results confirm those displayed in *Restaurants*. Although there is no clear-cut style-shift and levels of standardness are consistently high in both 2nd (97.7% to the Italians and 100% to the British) and 3rd generation informants (75% to the Italians and 100% to the British), as Table 3-26 and Figure 3-19 present, the 3rd person present tense –s absence in the 3rd generation results when interacting with Italian interlocutors (25%) displays an unexpected level of non-standardness.

Table 3-26. Presence/absence of third person zero verbal person marking: detailed index of tokens for each occurrence in the *Seller* workplace dataset.

INTERLOCUTOR	ITALIAN			BRITISH		
GENERATION	1st	2nd	3rd	1st	2nd	3rd
+S	-	42	6	-	9	1
-S	-	1	2	-	-	-
TOTAL	-	43	8	-	9	1

The examples below are interesting instances of 3rd generation speech:

18) AN: Oh that's nice of her. She seem a nice lady, really cut in.
19) AN: I'll let you know. It leave, it depends on what time they're all here tomorrow night.

The levels of zero third person -s are interesting above all considering the standardness of 2nd generation BIs with regard to this variable in both *Restaurant* and *Seller* data. As suggested for the 3rd generation findings in the preceding workplace, third person –s seems to function here mainly as a marker of the 3rd generation group's identity of ethnicity and age.

Some significant findings become evident when style shift is verified based on audience design in the speech of 1st generation informants. A good example is given in the *Hairdresser* data.

Figure 3-19. Presence/absence of third person zero verbal person marking: detailed index of tokens for each occurrence in the *Seller* workplace dataset

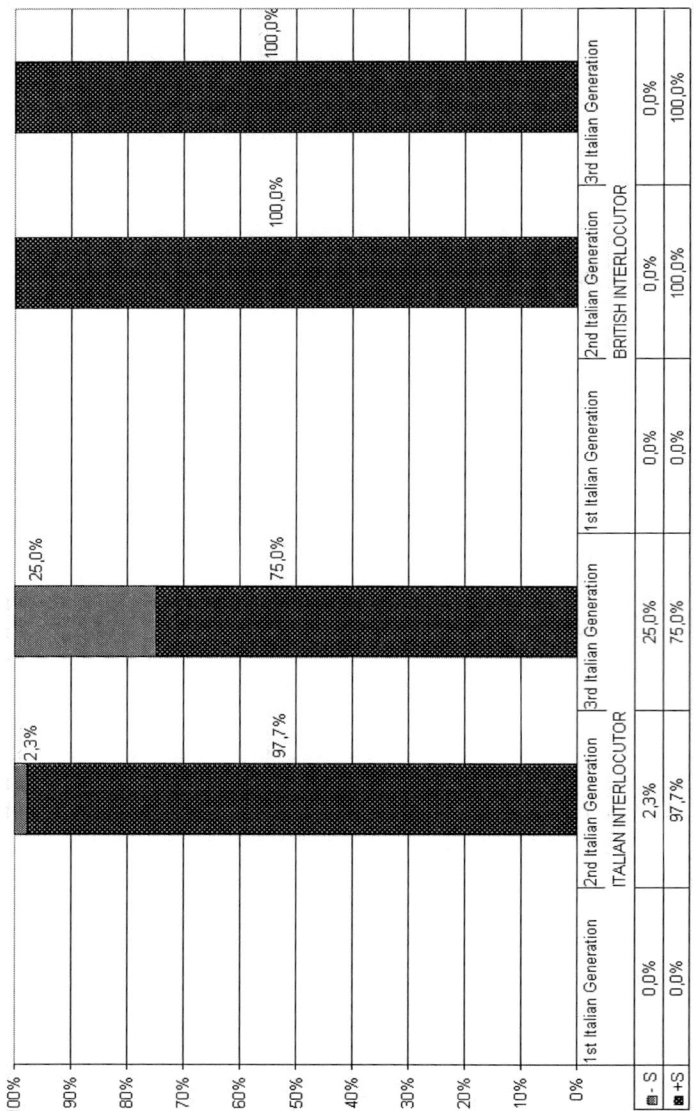

Lastly, the *Hairdresser* dataset reveals occurrences of mainly 1st generation BIs. As Table 3-27 and Figure 3-20 display, the highest levels of 3rd person present tense –s absence are found in the speech of 1st generation and in this audience type. Compared to 2nd and 3rd generations, these results show the highest levels of non-standardness.

Table 3-27. Presence/absence of third person zero verbal person marking: detailed index of tokens for each occurrence in the *Hairdresser* workplace dataset.

INTERLOCUTOR	ITALIAN			BRITISH		
GENERATION	1st	2nd	3rd	1st	2nd	3rd
+S	5	9	-	4	-	-
-S	8	-	-	17	-	-
TOTAL	13	9	-	21	-	-

Surprisingly, the interlocutor does not seem to have an effect on the behaviour of this variable. Informants reveal very remarkable levels of variation, both when speaking to Italian (61.5%) and British interlocutors (81%), whereas 2nd generation informants proved to be very standard again in this data set (100%).

Let us see some examples of 1st generation tokens extracted from the encounters with Italian interlocutors.

20) V: Eh, what *he say*, you must cut some off!
21) V: Which *one come* with me?
22) V: *This look* like a terrorist [...]

Clear-cut instances are also found when the interlocutor is British, as in the examples below:

23) TO: Yeah, forty nine years old. She, *she don't?* *believe* you.
24) TO: Eh, but, I tell you that otherwise, *who pay* me.

Figure 3-20. Presence/absence of third person zero verbal person marking: detailed
index of tokens for each occurrence in the *Hairdresser* workplace dataset.

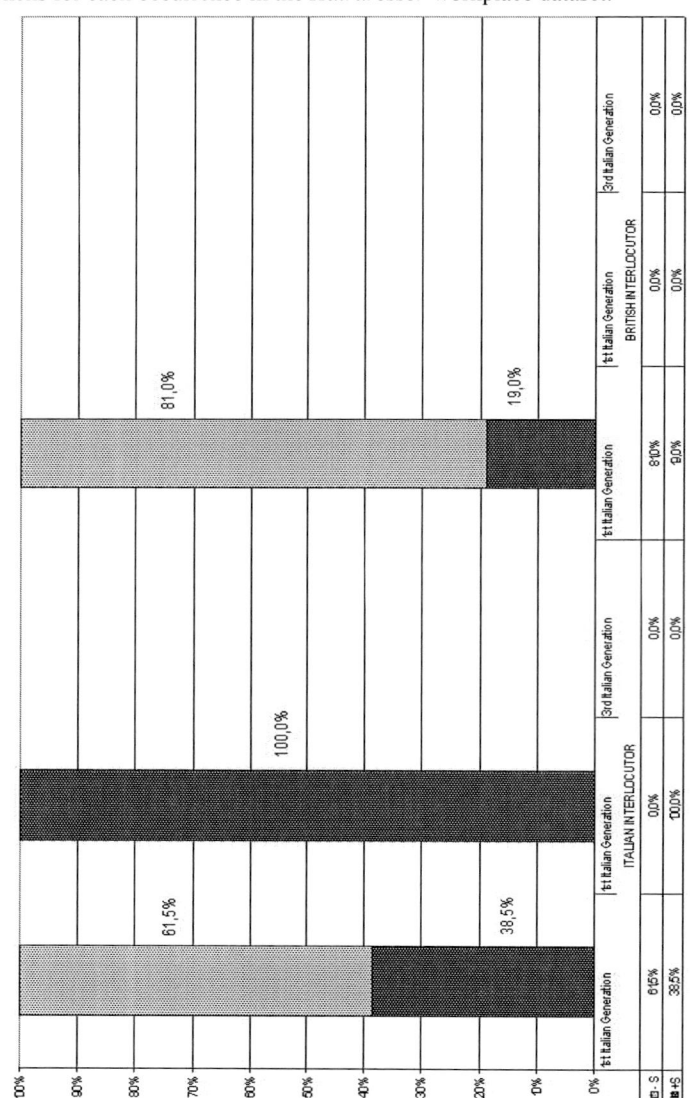

These patterns conform with the interpretation of 1st generation hairdressers given so far. Unlike the 3rd generation findings, although both show consistent levels of zero third person marking, the reasons are arguably different. First generation informants working in the hairdressing field do not seem to use this feature as a marker of group identity, and in this case findings rather confirm a transfer from L1 to the informants' L2 variety of English.

3.6 Some observations on methods and results

The interpretations offered in the paragraph above are suggestions and possible explanations of the informants' patterns. Some limitations became evident during data analysis which were mainly due to the size of samples of speech produced by some informants in certain cases, or to a lesser role in the interaction. As mentioned above and in the previous chapter, these disadvantages are to be attributed to the ethnographic method adopted. When attempting to collect the most naturalistic data possible, there are inevitable disavantages. A decision was taken at the outset: primary importance was to be given to language use in the context of a range of interlocutors of different nationalities and ethnicities, as well as to a variety of workplace settings. In order to do so, an attempt was made to elicit the most natural and spontaneous workplace language. Interactions had to be protected from any contamination and take priority over predetermined research patterns, despite being prejudicial to a standardised framework which could allow more control over the data. The aim is to study how a speech community really behaves in everyday life and therefore the informants cannot be expected to follow a script or to be guided through the investigation step by step. The negative consequences are that some cells in the analysis may be empty or display fewer tokens, but this is because they are not always perfectly balanced for generation and interlocutor ethnicity. Rather than considering the incomplete data as a methodological failure, the investigation should be viewed as a successful attempt at impartial observation of real life interactions of Bedford Italians.

Just as some expected patterns are found for some informants on one variable and may be paralleled by other regular variables, lesser uniformity may also be achieved, for which parallels will have to be found elsewhere in the dataset. As is common to a lot of research, some variables form patterns confirming those hypothesized at the outset, while others do not. Researchers attempt to formulate plausible explanations for the phenomena they witness, but in some cases, some variables follow no pattern at all, and cannot always be clarified. If we take into consideration the sociolinguist's core question, '*Why* did *this speaker* say it *this way* on *this occasion?*', findings showing either accommodation or non-accommodation, reveal an answer. Speakers do not necessarily intentionally dissociate themselves from others, so even what seems to be a non-result is actually a result. For instance, Bell and Johnson's study (1997 as in Bell 2001) about Maori and Pakeha speakers shows how for a Pakeha male informant "his unhesitating production of Anglicised pronunciations seems to indicate unconsciousness of the options rather than deliberate choice of the Pakeha one". As Bell (2001) argues, the limitations of his audience design approach lie in the unpredictability of individual speakers who sometimes display an initiative use of style to express their identity, for which an integrating audience and a referee design come to their aid. One of the main critiques of the audience design approach, and other similar methods, lies in the assumption that there is a risk of reducing the complexity of speakers' language. In contrast, one of the advantages of the audience design Bell first proposed in 1984 is "its falsifiability" (Bell, 2001), for which predictions and presuppositions can be proved wrong. As far as results are concerned, proving these predictions and suppositions wrong would be as valid as proving them right.

Italian = Neapolitan dialect

CONCLUSIONS

"Language is constantly being made and remade by speakers in terms of their situation, need, interlocutor, audience, knowledge of other 'languages', and general strategies of communication". (Mesthrie and Bhatt 2008:7)

The Italian diaspora has involved complex and multidirectional language dynamics, and to account for the sociolinguistic processes that have taken place, this has had to be observed from many different perspectives.

The objective of this study in particular was to carry out a sociolinguistic examination of English in service encounters, providing some empirical data on the language behaviour of three generations of Italian residents in Bedford. Bell's audience design approach (2001) and accommodation theory were applied during the actual data analysis and, as discussed in Chapter 4, interesting patterns have emerged.

In general, most of the BIs tend to use their workplace language to accommodate to the audience: towards native-like pronunciation of Italian lexis while addressing Italians, and English pronunciation while addressing the British. They appear to adapt their language to that of the interlocutor, who is generally a customer in this context. By adapting and adjusting their language with regard to the situation, i.e. a service encounter context, and to the purpose, i.e. selling, as well as accommodating the addressees, their style appears to shift according to the specific business aims. Informants seem to adopt a British pronunciation with British customers who are more likely to prefer a British address, and vice versa. We can therefore infer that "phonological code-switching" exists for Bedford Italians when they shift and mix their pronunciation according to their purposes in the workplace. Through audience design, speakers apply a range of linguistic resources which they have at their disposal in their speech community–which in the case of the BI community means relying on two languages, Italian and English, both part of the community and the interlocutor's (passive) repertoire – and strategically respond to different kinds of audience, in order to consciously or unconsciously reach an objective.

An investigation took place of five linguistic variables in the speech of three BI generations in three service encounters which were labelled *Restaurants*, *Sellers* and *Hairdressers*. Two of these are phonological, examined from two related angles, i.e. *foreign (a)* (typical of words such as *pasta*, *lasagne*, and *latte,* for instance) which was selected and analysed with a frequently occurring cluster of phonemes, isolated in Italian words when code-switched into English, and which could reveal Anglicisation. Three others are morphological: (1) plurality in Anglicised Italian lexis, (2) the presence/absence of inversion in question formation, and (3) the presence/absence third person zero in verbal person marking.

To sum up the above findings, in most cases, audience design seems to influence the language and repertoires within the speech of the Bedford Italian community, in which there not only seem to be switches from one language to another, but also style shifts in the linguistic repertoire. It was shown that BI informants displayed different numbers of occurences of the features with different interlocutors in different settings.

Regarding the 1st generation, lower levels of accommodation were shown than in the 2nd and 3rd generations. The 1st generation is the least likely to accommodate the interlocutor, and English is most definitely an L2 for them. This is true above all for those working in barber shops and hairdressers. Very rarely do they Anglicise in the hairdressing field, and although there is a slight shift towards Anglicisation when the addressee is British, it is in this group that the most consistent display of features identified as Italian are to be found. The fact that their pronunciation is fully Italian was confirmed by the foreign /a/ analysis which reveals a clear Italian-oriented quality of their /a/ sounds. What seems to be in contrast with this trend, but actually conforms with the interpretation predicted by audience design, are the results of 1st generation informants in the *Restaurants* dataset, in which some quite significant levels of Anglicisation (34.3%) are found when the addressee is Italian. This result concurs with the Style Axiom, using Bell's terms (1984, 2001:145), according to which "inter-relation between intra-speaker style shift and inter-speaker language differences is a derivation". Bell claims that "Variation on the style dimension within the speech of *a single speaker derives from and echoes the variation which exists between speakers on the 'social' dimension.*" (2001:145 my emphasis). Therefore, variation within the speech of one *Restaurant* 1st generation informant can represent the variation of that type of service encounter. Other reasons may lie in the type of migration 1st generation speakers belong to. The *Restaurant* informants arrived in town with the second flow of immigrants in the 1960s, whereas the *Hairdresser* informants mainly belong to the first migration flow in the 1950s, so it can be hypothesised that differences in 1st generation patterns may also be a consequence of their migration background.

When considering morphological features, 1st generation informants in the hairdressing trade form plural nouns of Italian origin either by using regular English patterns or Italian plural structures which are uttered in a code-switched situation. In the *Restaurant* dataset, on the other hand, some mixed forms of plurality emerge, showing a significant degree of accommodation according to the interlocutor's ethnicity. In addition to the morphology of the 1st generation, non-inverted questions and third person zero marking appear to characterise their speech, therefore showing the highest rating of non-standardness. An overall explanation for all the features analysed could lead us to see L2 errors in the interlingua of 1st generation informants as more likely than any other reason.

Probably the clearest patterns are those of 2nd generation informants who seem to accommodate a great deal to their audience. In each of the workplaces, these informants appear to adopt Italian pronunciation towards Italians and English-oriented pronunciation to the British. More specifically, the highest levels of accommodation to their audience are found in the *Restaurants* dataset. In that work setting, 2nd generation BIs Anglicise less when addressing an Italian interlocutor (30%), in contrast with the levels of Anglicisation displayed when addressing a British interlocuter (75.7%). Their ratings become even more marked regarding the articulation of foreign /a/. When it comes to this particular variable, the informants seem to disregard both the British back allophone [ɑ:] which is preferred less frequently(17.3%), and the [æ] variant (2.5%) to an Italian interlocutor, in favour of the front Italian phone [a] which is articulated most frequently (80.2%). On the other hand, when addressing a British interlocutor, higher levels of Anglicisation are found and informants display a much stronger preference for the British allophone [ɑ:] (92.3%). Both the *Seller* and the *Hairdresser* datasets confirm the trend of 2nd generation BIs with regard to Anglicisation and foreign /a/.

Less clear-cut results are found, however, regarding morphological variables. Second generation BIs working in the field of sales and addressing Italian interlocutors, form the plurals of Italian nouns using more mixed forms (66.7%) than those working in restaurants (31.3%), similarly showing quite a significant use of mixed plurals when communicating with British interlocutors as well. In this case, audience design seems to apply less in their speech, or at least there seems to be less accommodation. On the other hand, findings regarding 2nd generation hairdressers report a very standard usage of both question formation and third person verbal marking, in spite of quite a remarkable level of non-standardness found in the speech of 2nd generation informants working in the other two workplaces. Although 3rd person present tense –s is not very widespread in the speech of informants in either the *Seller* (2.3%) or *Restaurant* (3.7%) datasets, non-standard non-inverted questions show higher levels of usage are preferred when communicating with Italians (9.3% and 10.1% respectively) than with the British (1.7% and 3.3% correspondingly), therefore confirming degrees of accommodation, as predicted by audience design.

Last but not least, 3rd generation BIs display the most interesting and challenging findings that require an explanation. Apart from the hairdressing workplace where no occurrences emerged, the *Restaurants* and the *Sellers* reveal consistent levels of variation. Surprisingly, in the *Restaurant* dataset, Anglicisation of Italian lexis seems to be preferred when speaking to Italian (54.5%) rather than British (40%) interlocutors, therefore showing less accommodation, an upturned audience design, and also behaving unlike either 1st or 2nd generations. In this case, it is worth noting that a mixed pronunciation which stands mid-way is preferred in 30% of cases when speaking to a British interlocutor. Anglicisation is confirmed by the articulation of foreign /a/, for which, while addressing an Italian interlocutor, both British allophones [ɑ:] and [æ] (41.9% and 18.5% respectively) are preferred to the Italian front [a] (39.6% only), whereas [ɑ:] predominates (66.7%) when the addressee is British, and [a] is produced only 33.3% of the time. In contrast with these results, the pronunciation *in Sellers* is closer to previous generations who largely Italianise (56.7%) Italian lexis while communicating with Italian interlocutors, articulating foreign /a/ with [a] on most occasions (63.2%). Explanations could lie in the intermediate pronunciation that 3rd generation informants adopt. In spite of the widespread use of the Italian allophone [a], mixed pronunciations include (non)-aspiration of plosives and FACE vowels, which have been investigated in previous work carried out on 3rd generation BIs (Guzzo 2005, 2007), and which reveal a significant level of non-standard articulations which could not be fully explained through an Italian L1 influence. In contrast with their parents' generation, 3rd generation speech and accent appeared closer to Bangladeshi and other minority groups than to Italians. For this reason, the rather widespread use of mixed pronunciation in the present dataset could be linked to the same trend, therefore showing that an increasing feeling of "non-Britishness" could be reflected in their speech and in less accommodation to the British. These findings have been reinforced by a forthcoming preliminary study of 3rd generation Peterborough Italians conducted by Guzzo in 2011, which found that features such as the de-aspiration of syllable-initial and pre-vocalic plosive sounds confirm the creation of an *"in-code"* which is common among 3rd generation Anglo-Italians in England as well as other minority groups.

As for the morphological variables, plurality of Italian lexis shows quite an interesting pattern in which regular English plural forms are preferred whether the addressee is Italian (50%) or British (100%). Nonetheless, a substantial amount of mixed plurals (42.8%) are also used by 3rd generation informants in the *Restaurant* dataset. Third person present tense –s absence, on the other hand, is significantly higher in the speech of 3rd generation informants than in that of their 2nd generation parents. When the addressee is Italian, with regard to both restaurants and sales workplaces, third person –s tends to be omitted (26.3% and 25% respectively), whereas standard usage is reported while communicating to a British interlocutor (100%). Lastly, question formation requires us to be even more reflective. Partially conforming with the interpretation of Anglicisation, the usage of non-standard non-inverted questions shows that 3rd generation BIs, addressing Italian interlocutors, form fewer non-standard questions when working in *Restaurants* (4.5%) than in sales (16.1%). Interestingly, when addressing a British interlocutor, they display both a standard inverted and non-inverted question formation in sales (66.7% and 33.3% respectively), which means no tokens of non-standard non-inverted use are found in the *Seller* dataset, while a higher usage of non-standard question formation (9.1%) is found in *Restaurants*. Again, an explanation for these patterns can lie in the 3rd generation's need to assert themselves and their identity though a departure from what represents Britishness; by showing variation, adopting some non-British as well as non-standard features of English, and accommodating less to British interlocutors, they are marking their "non-Britishness". The style shift of 3rd generation informants, in this case, is displayed through a conscious reflection on their identity rather than marking a precise group identity, as the age and generation of the informants becomes more distant from that of their grandparents. The linguistic features analysed operate, therefore, as ethnic identity markers, sometimes helping them assert and confirm their Italian heritage. Further to this, a study on the online use of an Anglo-Italian ethnolect, by Guzzo and Balirano in 2011, demonstrated the role of social networks in creating, maintaining and developing an "online Italian diasporic identity".

Discussing the findings generally, most of the BIs use their workplace language to accommodate to the audience: towards native-like pronunciation of Italian lexis while addressing Italians, and English pronunciation while addressing the British. This use of (non)-Anglicisation seems to be exploited for business purposes. In other words, BIs appear to adapt their language to that of the interlocutor, who is generally a customer. Adapting and adjusting their language with regard to the situation, i.e. a service encounter context, and the purpose, i.e. selling, as well as accommodating the addressees, their style appears to shift according to the specific business aims. In other words, the informants seem to adopt a British pronunciation with British customers who are more likely to prefer a British address, and vice versa. In that sense, the strategic use of language is confirmed. Through audience design, speakers apply a range of the available linguistic resources in their speech community – which in the case of the BI community means relying on two languages, Italian and English, which are both part of the community and the interlocutor's (passive) repertoire – and strategically respond, consciously or unconsciously, to different types of audience in order to reach an objective.

This investigation of the Bedford Italian community has aimed to illustrate the correlation between the sociolinguistics of service encounters involving BIs and British interlocutors and leads to the question of further research. There is scope for a more detailed and in-depth study of the hybrid mechanisms of workplace language in Italian diaspora communities within an audience design framework. A contrastive analysis between casual conversations and business discourse could be taken into consideration for example, as well as a sociolinguistic study comparing the BI speech community with other Italian communities in Britain. This will hopefully lead one day to a well-structured and fully documented definition of *Italian-English* varieties spoken by Italians across the UK.

BIBLIOGRAPHY

Alladina, Safder and Viv Edwards. *Multilingualism in the British isles.* London and New York: Longman, 1991.

Agar, Michael H. *The professional stranger: An informal introduction to ethnography.* San Diego: Academic Press, 1996.

Alam, Farhana. *Language and identity in "Glaswesian" adolescents.* MLitt dissertation. Glasgow: University of Glasgow, 2007.

Baker, Philip, and John Eversley. *Multilingual Capital.* London: Battlebridge Publications, 2000.

Bakhtin, Michail. *The Dialogic Imagination.* Edited by Michael Holquist, translated by Caryl Ermerson and Michael Holquist. Austin: University of Texas Press, 1981.

—. "The Problem of Speech Genres". In *Speech Genre of Other Late Essays,* edited by Caryl Emersen and Michael Holquist, 60-102. Austin, TX: University of Texas Press, 1986.

Balirano, Giuseppe, and Siria Guzzo. "Ethnic representation as a means of identity formation in Computer Mediated Cross-Communication". In *CLAVIER 09 – Corpus Linguistics and Language Variation,* edited by M. Bondi, S. Cacchiani, G. Palumbo, 137-162. R.I.L.A., Anno XLIII nn. 1-2-. Roma: Bulzoni Editori, 2011.

Bhatia, Vijay J. *Analysing Genre: Language Use in Professional Settings.* London: Longman, 1993.

Bell, Allan. "Language Style as Audience Design". *Language in Society* 13 (1984): 145-204.

—. "Back in Style: Reworking Audience Design". In *Style and Sociolinguistic Variation,* edited by Penelope Eckert and John R. Rickford, 139-169. Cambridge: Cambridge University Press, 2001.

Bettoni, C. and J. Gibbons. "Linguistic Purism and Language Shift: A Guise.Voice Study of the Italian Community in Sydney". In *The Future of Ethnic Languages in Australia. International Journal of the Sociology of Language,* edited by A. Pauwels. Special Issue, 12. Berlin: De Gruyter, 1988.

Blom, Jan-Petter, and John Gumperz. "Social Meaning in Linguistic Structures: Code-Switching in Norway." In *Directions in Sociolinguistics: The Ethnography of Communication,* edited by John

J. Gumperz, and Dell H. Hymes, 407-434. Oxford: Basil Blackwell, 1972.

Boberg, Charles. *Variation and change in the nativization of foreign (a) in English.* Published Ph.D. dissertation, University of Pennsylvania: Penn Libraries, 1997.

Boissevain, Jeremy. *Friends of Friends: Networks, Manipulators and Coalitions.* Oxford: Basil Blackwell, 1974.

Britain, David. *Surviving 'Estuary English': innovation diffusion, koineisation and local dialect differentiation in the English Fenland.* Essex research report in Linguistics, 2002.

Britain, David, and Kazuko Matsumoto. *Contact and obsolescence in a diaspora variety of Japanese: The case of Palau in Micronesia.* Essex research report in Linguistic, 2003.

Britain, David. "Introduction". In *Language in the British Isles,* edited by David Britain, 1-6. Cambridge: Cambridge University Press, 2007.

——. "Grammatical variation in England". In *Language in the British Isles,* edited by David Britain, 75-104. Cambridge: Cambridge University Press, 2007.

Brook, G.L.. *English Dialects.* 2nd edn. London: Andre Deutsch, 1963.

Brown, Penelope, and Stephen Levinson. *Politeness: Some Universals of Language Use.* Cambridge: Cambridge University Press, 1987.

Brown, R. and M. Ford. "Address in American English". *Journal of Abnormal and Social Psychology* 62 (1961): 375-385. Also appeared in *Communication in Face to face Interaction,* edited by J. Laver and S. Hutcheson. Harmondsworth: Penguin Books, 1972.

Brown, Roger, and Albert Gilman. "The Pronouns of Power and Solidarity". In *Style in Language,* edited by Thomas A. Sebeok, 253-77. Cambridge Mass.: MIT Press, 1960.

Candlin, Christopher N., and Maurizio Gotti (edited by). *Intercultural Aspects of Specialized Communication.* Bern: Peter Lang, 2004.

Cavallaro, Renato. *Storie senza Storia. Indagine sull'emigrazione calabrese in Gran Bretagna.* Roma: Centro Studi Emigrazione, 1981.

Cervi, Bruno. "The Italian speech community". In *Multlingualism in the British Isles 1: the Older Mother Tongues and Europe,* edited by Safder Alladina and Viv Edwards, 214-227. London: Longman, 1991.

Chambers, Jack K. *Sociolinguistic theory.* Oxford: Blackwells, 1995.

——. "Patterns of Variation including Change". In *The Handbook of Language Variation and Change,* edited by Jack K. Chambers, Peter Trudgill and Natalie Schilling-Estes, 349-372. Oxford: Blackwell Publishing, 2004.

Cheshire, Jenny. *Variation in an English Dialect: A Sociolinguistic Study.* Cambridge: Cambridge University Press, 1982.

Cheshire, Jenny, Paul Kerswill, Sue Fox and Eivind Torgersen. "Contact, the feature pool and the speech community: the emergence of multicultural London English". *Journal of Sociolinguistics* 15 (2011): 151-196.

Chomsky, Noam. "On WH-Movement". In *Formal Syntax*, edited by Peter Culicover, Thomas Wasow, and Adrian Akmajian, 71–132. New York: Academic Press, 1977.

Clark, Herbert H., and T. B. Carlson, "Hearers and Speech Acts". *Language* 58 (1982): 332-73.

Colpi, Terri. *Italians forward.* London: Mainstream Publishers, 1991.

Colucci, Michele. "L'emigrazione Italiana in Gran Bretagna nel Secondo Dopoguerra: il Caso di Bedford (1951-60)". *Journal of Dimensioni e Problemi della Ricerca Storica*, 1 (2002): 253-272.

Corder, S.P. "The significance of learners' errors". *International Review of Applied Linguistics* 5 (1967): 161-169.

Coupland, Nikolas. "Style-shifting in a Cardiff Work Setting". *Language in Society* 9 (1980): 1-12.

—. *Dialect in Use: Sociolinguistic Variation in Cardiff English.* Cardiff: University of Wales Press, 1988.

—. *Style.* Cambridge: Cambridge University Press, 2007.

Coupland, Nikolas, and Virpi T. Ylänne-McEwen. "Talk about the Weather: Small Talk, Leisure Talk and Travel Industry". In *Small talk,* edited by J. Coupland, 163-182. Harlow: Longman, 2000.

De Mauro, Tullio. *Storia Linguistica dell'Italia Unita.* 2nd edn. Bari: Laterza, 1970.

De Villiers, Jill. G. and Valerie E. Johnson. "The information in third-person /s/: acquisition across dialects of American English". *Journal of Child Language*, 34 (2007): 133-158.

Drew Paul, and John Heritage. *Talk at work: interaction in institutional settings.* Cambridge University Press, 1992.

Dudley-Evans, Tony, and Magie J. St. John. *Development in English for Specific Purposes, a Multi-disciplinary Approach.* Cambridge: Cambridge University Press, 1998.

Duranti, Alessandro, and Charles Goodwin (edited by) *Rethinking Context: Language as an Interactive Phenomenon.* Cambridge University Press, 1992.

Eckert, Penelope. *Linguistic variation as social practice.* Blackwell Publishers, 2000.

Ervin-Tripp, Susan. *Language Acquisition and Communicative Choice.* Stanford: Stanford University Press, 1973.

Fairclough, Norman. *Analysing Discourse.* London and New York: Routledge, 2003.

Feagin, Crawford. "Entering the community: Fieldwork". In *The Handbook of Language Variation and Change,* edited by Jack K. Chambers, Peter Trudgill and Natalie Schilling-Estes, 20-39. Oxford: Blackwell Publishing, 2004.

Fischer, Claude S.. *To Dwell Among Friends: Personal Networks in Town and City.* Chicago: University of Chicago Press, 1982.

Foulkes, Paul and Gerard Docherty. *Urban voices.* London: Arnold, 1999.

Fox, Sue. *Linguistic and Sociocultural Contact in London's East End: the Bangladeshi presence.* Paper presented at the conference on Consequences of Mobility: Linguistic and Sociocultural Contact Zones, Roskilde 23rd – 24th May 2003.

—.*The demise of 'Cockneys'?: Language change in London's 'traditional' East End.* Unpublished PhD dissertation. Colchester: University of Essex, 2007.

Fortier, Anne-Marie. *Migrant Belongings. Memory, Space, Identity.* Oxford: Berg, 2000.

Giles, Howard. "Accent mobility: A model and some data". *Anthropological Linguistics* 15(1973): 87-105.

Giles, Howard, and Peter Powesland. *Speech Style and Social Evaluation.* London: Academic Press, 1975.

Goffman, Erving. *The Presentation of Self in Everyday Life.* New York: Doubleday, 1959.

—. *Forms of Talk.* Oxford: Blackwell, 1981.

Gotti, Maurizio. *Specialized discourse: linguistic features and changing conventions.* Bern: Peter Lang, 2003.

Gumperz, John J. *Discourse Strategies.* Cambridge: Cambridge University Press, 1982.

Guzzo, Siria. *Language Shift: the case of the Bedford Italian Community.* Unpublished MA dissertation. Colchester: University of Essex, 2005.

—. "Multilingualism and Language Variation in the British Isles: the Case of the Bedford Italian Community". In *Discourse Analysis and Contemporary Social Change,*edited by Norman Fairclough, Giuseppina Cortese and Patrizia Ardizzone, 233-257. Bern: Peter Lang, 2007.

—. "Bedford Italians: Morphosyntax and code-switching for ethnic identity". In *Le comunità immigranti nel Regno Unito: il caso di*

Bedford, edited by Adam Ledgeway & Anna Laura Lepschy, 97-118. Perugia: Guerra, 2011.

Guzzo, Siria and Anna Gallo. "Migration and Multilingualism in the UK: the case of the Italian communities in Bedford and Peterborough". In *Multilinguismo in contesto transnazionale. Metodologie e progetti di ricerca sulle dinamiche linguistiche degli italiani all'estero*, edited by Margherita Di Salvo, Paola Moreno, Rosanna Sornicola, 81-112. Roma: Aracne, 2013.

Guzzo, Siria, Sue Fox and David Britain. *From L2 to ethnic dialect: hiatus resolution strategies across the generations in Bedford Italian English.* Essex research report in Linguistics, Forthcoming.

Hagège, Claude. *L'enfant aux Deux Langues (The child between two languages).* Paris: Odile Jacob, 1996.

Halliday, M.A.K.. "Linguistic Function and Literary Style: An Inquiry into the Language of William Golding's *The Inheritors*". In *The Stylistic Reader: from Roman Jabobson to the Present,* edited by J.J.Weber, 56-91. London: Arnold, 1996.

Harris, Roxy, and Ben Rampton. *The Language, Ethnicity and Race Reader.* London and New York: Routledge, 2003.

Hasan, Ruqaiya. "The Structure of a Text". In *Language, Context and Text: Aspects of a Language in a Social-Semiotic Perspective,* edited by M.A.K. Halliday and Ruqaiya Hasan, 52-69. Cambridge: Cambridge University Press, 1985.

Hymes, Dell. "Models of the Interaction of Language and Social Life". In *Directions in Sociolinguistics: the Ethnography of Communication,* edited by John J. Gumperz and Dell. Hymes, 35-71. New York: Holt, Rinehart and Winston, 1972.

—. *Foundations in Sociolinguistics.* Philadelphia: University of Pennsylvania Press, 1974.

Hock, Hans Henrich. *Principles of Historical Linguistics.* Berlin: Mouton de Gruyter, 1986.

Holmes, Janet and Miriam Meyerhoff. "The Community of Practise: Theories and Methodologies in Language and Gender Research". *Language in Society* 28 (1999):173-183.

Holmes, Janet and Maria Stubbe. *Power and Politeness in the Workplace.* London: Pearson Education, 2003.

Houtkoop, Hanneke. *Interaction and the standardized survey interview: the living questionnaire.* Cambridge: Cambridge University Press, 2000.

Hudson, R.A. *Sociolinguistics.* Cambridge University, 2001.

Jackson, B. *Fieldwork.* Urbana: University of Illinois, 1987.

Johnstone, Barbara. *Qualitative Methods in Sociolinguistics*. Sage Publications, 2000.

Khan, Arfaan. *A Sociolinguistic Study of Birmingham English: Language Variation and Change in a Multi-Ethnic British Community*. Unpublished PhD dissertation. Lancaster: Lancaster University, 2007.

King, Russell. "Italian Migration to the UK". *Geography* 62 (1977):176-186.

King, R., and P.D. King. "The Spatial Evolution of the Italian community in Bedford". *East Midland Geographer*, 6 (1977): 337-345.

Kyambi, Sarah. *Beyond Black and White: Mapping new immigrant communities*. London: IPPR, 2005a.

—. *New Immigrant Communities: New Integration Challenges?* London: Institute for Public Policy Research, 2005b.

Koch, P. "Lexical Typology from a Cognitive and Linguistic Point of View". In: *Lexicology: An International on the Nature and Structure of Words and Vocabularies/Lexikologie: Ein internationales Handbuch zur Natur und Struktur von Wörtern und Wortschätzen*, edited by D. Alan Cruse *et alt.*, 1142-1178. Berlin/New York: Walter de Gruyter, 2002.

Koester, Almut. "Relational Sequences in Workplace Genres". *Journal of Pragmatics* 36 (2004): 1405-28.

—. *Investigating Workplace Discourse*. London and New York: Routledge, 2006.

Labov, William. "The social motivation of a sound change". *Word* 19 (1963): 273-309.

—. *The Social Stratification of English in New York City*. Washington, DC: Centre of Applied Linguistics, 1966/2006.

—. *Sociolinguistic Patterns*. Philadelphia: Pennsylvania University Press, 1972.

—. *The Significance of Marginal Phonemes*. Paper presented to NWAVE 2. Washington, DC, 1973.

—. "Field methods of the project on linguistic change and variation". In *Language in Use: Readings in Sociolinguistics*, edited by J. Baugh and J. Sherzer, 28-66. Englewood Cliffs, NJ: Prentice Hall, 1984.

—.*Principles of linguistic change*. Oxford: Blackwell, 1994 .

Lakkis, Khadija and Mirna Abdel Malak. "Understanding the Transfer of Prepositions". *FORUM,* 38 (2000). (Online edition: http://exchanges.state.gov/forum/vols/vol38/no3/p26.htm)

Lampi, M. *Linguistic Components of Strategy in Business Negotiations*. Helsinki: Helsinki School of Economics, 1986.

Maiden, Maiden, and Mair Parry. *The dialect of Italy*. London and New York: Routledge, 1997.

Lave, Jean and Etienne Wenger. *Situated Learning: Legitimate Peripheral Participation*. Cambridge: Cambridge University Press, 1991.

Maingueneau, D. "Analysing Self-Constituting Discourses". *Discourse Studies*. 1/2 (1999): 175-199.

Matsumoto, Kazuko. *Language Contact and Change in Micronesia: Evidence from the Multilingual Republic of Palau*. PhD Dissertation. University of Essex, 2002.

McCarthy, M. "Mutually Captive Audiences: Small Talk and Close Contact Service Encounters". In *Small talk*, edited by J. Coupland, 84-109. Harlow: Longman, 2000.

Mesthrie, Rajend and Rakesh M. Bhatt. *World English*. Cambridge: Cambridge University Press, 2008.

Milroy, Lesley. *Language and Social Networks*. Oxford: Blackwell, 1987.

Milroy, Lesley and Matthew Gordon. *Sociolinguistics: Method and Interpretation*. Oxford: Blackwell, 2003.

Mitchell, T.F. "The Language of Buying and Selling in Cyrenaica: A Situational Statement". *Hésperis* 44(1957): 31-71. Reprinted in *Principles of Firthian Linguistics*, edited by T.F. Mitchell, 167-200. London: Longman, 1975.

Nguyen, Thanh Ha. *First Language Transfer and Vietnamese Learners' Oral Competence in English Past Tense Marking: A Case Study*. Master of Education (TESOL) Research Essay. Victoria, Australia: La Trobe University, 1995.

Palmer, Robert. "The Italians: Patterns of Migration in London". In *Between Two Cultures. Migrants and Minorities in Britain,* edited by James L. Watson, 242−268. Oxford: Basil, 1977.

Ragan, Sandra L. "Sociable Talk in Women's Healthcare Contexts: Two Forms of Non-Medical Talk". In *Small talk,* edited by J. Coupland, 269-87. Harlow: Longman, 2000.

Rampton, Ben. "Speech Community". In *Handbook of Pragmatics,* edited by Jef Verschueren, Jan-Ola Östman, Jan Blommaert and Chris Bulcaen, 1-34. Amsterdam: John Benjamins, 2000.

Reynolds, Mike and Mohammed Akram. "The maintenance of Punjabi and Urdu in Sheffield". In *Sociolinguistic and psycholinguistic perspectives on maintenance and loss of minority languages*, edited by Tom Ammerlaan, Madeleine Hulsen, Heleen Strating and Kutlay Yagmur, 249-265. Münster: Waxmann, 2001.

Romaine, Suzanne. *Language in society: an introduction to sociolinguistics*. Oxford: Oxford University Press, 1994.

Ross, John Robert. *Constraints on Variables in Syntax*. Ph.D. thesis, Massachusetts Institute of Technology, 1967.

Rubino, Antonia. "Italian in Australia: past and new Trends". *Proceedings of Innovations in Italian teaching workshop*, 1-15. Briffith University, 2002.

Sacks, Harvey, Emanuel A. Schegloff and Gail Jefferson. "A Simplest Systematics for the Organization of Turn-Taking for Conversation". *Language* 50 (1974): 696-735.

Schilling-Estes, Natalie. "Investigating 'self-conscious' Speech: the Performance Register in Ocracoke English". *Language in Society* 27(1998): 53-83.

Scotton, Carol M.. "Diglossia and code-switching". In *The Fergusonian Impact* Vol 2, edited by Joshua A. Fishman *et al*, 403-417. Berlin: Mouton de Gruyter, 1986.

Sharma, D. "Style repertoire and social change in British Asian English". *Journal of Sociolinguistics* 15(2011): 464-492.

Shuy, R., W. Wolfram and W. Riley. *Linguistic correlates of social stratification in Detroit speech*. Final Report: Cooperative Research Project No. 6-1347, United States Office of Education, 1967.

Siewierska, Anna. "Third-person zero of verbal person marking". In *World atlas of language structure*, edited by Martin Haspelmath, Matthew S. Dryer, David Gil and Bernard Comrie, 418-421. Oxford: Oxford University Press, 2005.

Silverman, David. *Doing Qualitative Research*. SAGE Publications, 2001.

Sponza, Lucio. *Italian Immigrants in Nineteenth-Century Britain: Realities and Images*. Leicester: Leicester University Press, 1988.

Stubbe, Maria and Janet Holmes. "Talking Maori or Pakena in English: signalling identity in discourse". In *New Zealand English*. John Benjamins Publishing Company, 1984.

Stubbs, Michael (edited by). *The other languages of England: Linguistic Minorities Project*. London: Routledge and Kegan Paul, 1985.

Swales, John. *Genre Analysis: English in Academic and Research Settings*. Cambridge: Cambridge University Press, 1990.

Thomason, Sarah Grey and Terrence Kaufman. *Language Contact, Creolization, and Genetic Linguistics*. Berkeley, Los Angeles, Oxford: University of California Press, 1988.

Torgersen, Eivind, Kerswill Paul and Sue Fox. "Ethnicity as a source of changes in the London vowel system". In *Language Variation - European Perspectives. Selected Papers from the Third International Conference on Language Variation in Europe (ICLaVE3), Amsterdam,*

June 2005, edited by Frans L. Hinskens, 249-263 Amsterdam: Benjamins, 2006.

Tosi, Arturo. *Immigration and bilingual education.* Pergamon Institute of English, 1984.

Trudgill, Peter. *The Social Differentiation of English in Norwich.* Cambridge: CUP, 1974.

—. *Dialects in Contact.* Oxford: Blackwell, 1986.

—. *Dialects.* London & New York: Routledge, 1994.

—. *Sociolinguistics: an introduction to language and society.* London: Penguin Books, 1995.

—. "Third person singular zero: African American vernacular English, East Anglian dialects and Spanish persecution in the Low Countries". *Folia Linguistica Historica* 18 (1998): 139-148.

—. *The dialects of England.* Oxford & Cambridge: Blackwell Publishers, 1999.

—. *Sociolinguistic variation and change.* Edinburgh: Edinburgh University Press, 2002.

Ventola, Eija. *The Structure of Social Action. A Systematic Approach to the Semiotics of Service Encounters.* London: Frances Pinter, 1987.

Ylänne-McEwen, Virpi T. *Relational Processes within a Transactional Setting: An Investigation of Travel Agency Discourse.* Unpublished PhD Thesis. Cardiff: University of Wales, 1996.

Yule. George. *Pragmatics.* Oxford: Oxford University Press, 1996.

Wenger, Etienne. *Community of Practice.* Cambridge: Cambridge University Press, 1998.

Wei, Li. *Three generations, Two languages, One family.* Clevedon, Avon: Multilingual Matters Ltd. 1984.

Weinreich, Uriel. *Languages in Contact: Findings and Problems.* The Hague: Mouton, 1968.

Zontini, Elisabetta. *Italian Families and Social Capital - Rituals and Provision of Care in British-Italian Transnational Families.* Series: Families & Social Capital ESRC Research Group Working Papers. London: London South Bank University, Faculty of Arts and Human Sciences, 2004.